GW00862990

My Incredible Innings

The 'old man' himself. No comment needed!

My Incredible Innings
W. E. (Bill) Alley

PELHAM BOOKS

First published in Great Britain by
PELHAM BOOKS LTD
26 Bloomsbury Street,
London, W.C.1
1969

© 1969 by W. E. Alley

All Rights Reserved. No part of this publication
may be reproduced, stored in a retrieval system,
or transmitted, in any form or by any means,
electronic, mechanical, photocopying, recording
or otherwise, without the prior permission of
the Copyright owner

7207 0305 0

Set and printed in Great Britain by Tonbridge
Printers Ltd, Peach Hall Works, Tonbridge,
Kent, in Times ten on twelve point, on paper
supplied by P. F. Bingham Ltd, Croydon, and
bound by James Burn at Esher, Surrey

Contents

Illustrations

ACKNOWLEDGEMENTS

Grateful acknowledgement is made to the following for the reproduction of the photographs indicated.

Press Association Photos: frontispiece, 14, 26
Blackpool Gazette: 11, 12, 13
Sport & General: 18, 25
Bristol Evening Post: 21
Bill Smith: 22
Harold King: 23
Northcliffe Newspapers: 24

Introduction

I talk an awful lot and that is why I'm writing this book. Well, it's one of the reasons. Another is that I can be talked into anything . . . on the cricket field, batting or bowling; in the dressing-room, walking along the pavement; and probably in my sleep I shouldn't wonder, I talk most of the time.

People have told me, and I've heard them telling others, 'Old Bill should write a book.' Well, I've fallen for it. If you are one of those who egged me on I hope you are satisfied! If, instead, you are one of the many thousands I've seen on hundreds of cricket grounds between Sydney and Somerset during the past thirty odd years – 'good on yer cobbers' for your encouragement in a wonderful life, and even if this book bores you to tears I hope you have shared some of the pleasure which cricket has given to me.

Now that I've started I'll take some stopping because what I'm actually doing is talking into a tape recorder and then when I know what I have said I'll write it all down!

All stories are supposed to start at the beginning, so I'm told. Well, I'll get around to that a little later. So much has happened since I started playing cricket that I could not deal here with everything even if it was all worthwhile.

Here and there I have achieved some fame, broken a few

records and, sometimes standing in the wings, I have been lucky enough to see really great players emerge and grow. Indeed, I've been around such a long time that I have been closer to the great personalities of the game more years than most observers.

To play first-class cricket is a privilege for the few. To have had *two* first-class careers is to have been particularly lucky. I have been even more fortunate. I have had three careers, each one lasting as long and perhaps longer than the majority of the privileged few who have played top cricket.

Don Bradman thought I was too old to begin a Test career with his Australian touring team visiting England in 1948. I had seen the writing on the wall a year before when I was denied a trip to New Zealand – so I packed my bags for my own trip to England to earn a few more bob before my career collapsed.

In the next ten years in the north country league cricket I began and enjoyed not only a new cricket career, but also a new life. The sun may not shine for so long or be so hot over Lancashire as it does along the Hawkesbury river, but I found just the same warmth in the welcome I got on the morning I arrived in a snowstorm.

You may never have heard of the Hawkesbury river, of course, and it is less likely that you will have heard of the Hawkesbury river bridge. I suppose that not many people give it a second glance, not even the members of the MCC tour parties when they cross it on their way from Sydney to Newcastle for the traditional three-day second-class match against Northern New South Wales. Next time I hope they'll doff their caps. It is the only memorial I'm likely to get. I helped to build it!

I'm proud to be known as 'Bill Alley, cricketer' but I was a pretty happy feller when I was labouring on an oyster farm, building that river bridge, being a railway fitter's mate, a blacksmith-striker and a dance hall bouncer. There was more to laugh than to cry about when rolling the wicket and cutting the grass and painting the seats and repairing the changing rooms and mending the nets . . . before changing from overalls into white flannels to play cricket for Colne or Blackpool.

I've been sad, too. Sometimes it didn't last long, like the

moment I realised that the Aussie cap which the public thought was mine was given to somebody else and I knew it was my last chance, gone. By the time you get to the end of this book you will know and understand why that moment of sadness passed. You will know why I would not now trade the life I have had in England for an Australian Test career.

My life as a county cricketer has given me more from the first-class game than I had a right to expect. At an age when most players retire, I was able to start! I have been given a place in the record books of English cricket which makes me a very proud man.

The stories I have chosen to tell about my three careers in cricket are concerned mainly with the time I have spent in England. This is now my home – and always will be so.

I hope to be walking the cricket fields of England for many years.

It is strange what tricks memory plays. I find it very difficult to recall the detail of my early life, even of my cricket successes. They say that early memories become clearer as you get older, proof to me that I am not so old as some people think!

However, for the time being I have to rely on odd scraps of paper and early cuttings to remind me of some things, and I had completely forgotten one of my first successes – until an old pamphlet came to light recently. It revealed that in the 1936–37 season W. Alley had a batting average of 125.4 for ten innings with a top score of 251 not out. That record by teenager Alley still stands in that Grade cricket.

Another old document which came to the surface at the same time still gives my ego a flip. As I give up playing the first-class game I hope that younger readers will forgive this revelation of my status on the other side of the world, a quarter of a century ago.

The document, headed 'Cricketing History of W. Alley' was published in 1943 and reads:

'Mr W. Alley who joined us this season . . .'

There is a summary of my figures, as a wicket-keeper (!), batsman, bowler and fielder, and reference that I had been acclaimed 'by the cricket fraternity as a worthy successor to Warren Bardsley'. I know how proud that made me feel.

The 'history' ends with a forecast. 'Much more should be heard of W. Alley in the post-war cricket era.'

I hope the historian was not referring to my talking . . . and I hope that you will find the story of my cricket has been worth telling. Please read on.

ONE

Fancy working at your age!

I'm fifty not out. It's written down on my birth certificate – which is just as well because I've a memory like a drain. I guess I had been playing first-class cricket for more than thirty years when I took to umpiring this summer.

I've never tried to hide my age but the more you tell the truth in this world, the more people disbelieve you. In fact, the 'Old Man Alley' saga has built up so much in recent years that I've begun to think it is time I drew my pension!

The jokers around the grounds reckoned people didn't go to see me play cricket. They went out of curiosity in case I dropped dead from exhaustion!

All this talk of *Anno Domini* doesn't worry me. W. G. Grace played for years and years – and he had a hell of a beard. They say I'm ancient, but I don't feel fifty. One of these days, I suppose, I am going to get the shock of my life. I might just crumple up and blow away to ashes. But right now I feel as fit as anyone on this earth.

It's incredible really. I started playing first grade cricket when Richie Benaud was a babe. Now Richie has put away his pads and I'm still in the game, umpiring six, seven days a week, and playing the occasional match.

My contemporaries in Australia were Bradman, Barnes and

O'Reilly, and last summer I played against a generation of Australians some of whom weren't even born when I started in cricket.

When people ask me what is the secret of my fitness, I tell them that I've been active all my life. I weigh around 14½ stone now and I can still get into my wedding suit. I don't need to diet, spend time in turkish baths or go off to a health farm to shed loads of fat. Three weeks before a cricket season starts I am usually about half-a-stone overweight and I can lose that without any trouble.

Exercise is the great thing. At my home near Taunton in Somerset, I do a lot of hunting, shooting and fishing. I also work in the garden. I have two acres of land and, while I could turn over the soil quicker with my rotary hoe, I prefer a spade. It makes me sweat, tones up the muscles and makes me feel better, especially after a binge!

Only the other day I thought to myself: Bill, mate, you're feeling sluggish after a heavy session in the local. It's the garden for you. So I threw on my old togs and my Wellington boots and cut knee high nettles for a couple of hours with a hook and scythe. That cleared away the cobwebs. You don't keep fit sitting around – and mechanical appliances can make you lazy.

During my time in cricket I have been accused of being a music-hall clown, umpire-baiter and a bad-tempered old bastard. I may be all those things, but I can honestly say I've never shirked a challenge. I've always tried to play the game to the best of my ability.

I've told people to get the hell out of it. I've often taken a rap for my pains. But I've no regrets. This game of cricket is my only way to the bank – and I've a wife and two kids to support.

It is no use playing any game half-heartedly, trying to do a first-class job with second-hand tools. And if you let the other feller stamp on you, you'll never get anywhere in this day and age.

They tell me only Hobbs and Woolley have scored more runs after the age of 40 than I did. I fancy the record is safe in this high pressure modern game. The pace is killing, and a lot of the fun has gone from the cricket. But youngsters need not be disheartened. Just let them follow the Alley rules for survival:

First – and most important: Keep your enthusiasm. I get the same kick out of a game as I did when they let us out of school to play in the yard back in Australia.

Second: Pick the right lass. I married a Lancashire girl and she's the greatest. She has stayed at home while I've gone off into the sun – and not complained. She knew this was the way we had to make our living.

Third: Keep yourself fit but don't be scared to have a couple of beers in the evening. It will help you unwind.

Cricket has always come first. I used to play Rugby League football and tennis, but cricket was always the backyard game as far as I was concerned. I can remember playing when I was so small that the other lads wouldn't let me bat. They were frightened I might get hurt.

Our cricket matches were staged on the cobbled streets near my home in the little oyster fishing village at Hawkesbury River, thirty-six miles from Sydney. We were a poor community, and I think I was the only boy wearing shoes out of a class of eighty at school.

Certainly, we could never afford proper cricket bats. Nine times out of ten we used a piece of paling or a roughly hewn lump of wood. Next day we sat in class with our hands covered in blisters and splinters of wood!

The ball used to fizz along at different heights, first to the left and then to the right. If you could plant a shot straight down the middle of the street, it would go for 100 yards.

I was an athletic type but not very big, and after a while I became the terror of the neighbourhood. I broke practically every window in the street with my sixes.

Dad was a local government employee and I was the oldest of a family of four boys and two girls.

One of my earliest and most vivid memories is of father's little red book in which he noted the form of racehorses. We knew it as the family bible, and as I got older he tried in vain to teach me the secrets of this form book. I must have gone without my dinner on more than one occasion because my father's betting habits had emptied the till. At any event, it laid the seeds of a life-long distaste of any form of gambling.

I was born in my grandmother's home and I wasn't very old when father and mother decided to move into their own house in another district. My dear grandmother greeted the news with typical forthrightness: 'If you go, he stops with me,' she told them. Afterwards, I used to visit my parents from time to time, but I was always back by nightfall.

My grandmother encouraged me in everything I did in sport. She used to fuss away, even up to the time when I started playing on matting wickets for the local club at Brookland. She would wrap up my one pair of snow-white pants, white shirt and shoes and say to me: 'For God's sake look after yourself – and don't get hurt.'

I can't recall anyone in the family being interested in cricket, although one of my brothers played Rugby League football. I picked up cricket as a game because this was our local sport in the little park at home.

At Brookland I developed a special style on the mat-covered concrete wickets. I never had any private coaching and we used to play in competitions at grounds up to about twenty-five miles distant.

I was very small but I had an uncanny eye. I used to whack the ball and whatever it looked like to the spectator, it was a great shot in my estimation.

My special pride at this time was clouting sixes. There was a shoe shop at a place called Hornsby which used to offer a pair of ordinary shoes if you scored a 100 wearing cricket boots bought from the shop. One particular season I collected no fewer than eleven pairs of shoes!

I left school at fifteen and my first job was on an oyster farm at Brookland. We started work at six in the morning, and our task was to wash and bottle the oysters ready for dispatch to Sydney. We earned about fifteen shillings a week – a lot of money in those days – and our big treat was a day out in Sydney. We would have a few beers, a couple of pies and perhaps go to a film. Then we caught the paper train home and thought we had had a smashing day.

I don't suppose many people know how oysters grow in Australia. They are cultivated on a mango stick, about five feet in length. These are put out in wired bundles on racks at a certain time in the season. The spawn from other oysters is caught under the sticks and eventually the young oyster begins to form. After the oyster has developed to about the size of the top of your finger, the wires are cut and the sticks separated and laid out on another frame.

These are long rows between two and three hundred yards in length, and the individual sticks are laid about eight inches apart on the battens. The young oysters on the sticks mature after about three years, when they are more or less saleable and ready to be opened. Our work was controlled by the tide. Some days you might go out and put the small oysters on the racks. Other days you would be opening and washing the mature oysters.

We used to find pearls, but they were very small and of no value. Of the thousands of oysters I have opened – I could open them at the rate of twenty-five an hour – I don't suppose I've seen more than eight or nine pearls. Nice little pearls but, as I say, of no value.

Later, I started work on a big road bridge across the Hawkesbury River. The bridge eventually carried traffic from Sydney to the North and was about the equivalent of a journey from London to Yorkshire. I did all sorts of manual jobs, working as a fitter and wheeling and mixing concrete. By this time I was beginning to learn the value of money and took a better paid job, working as a driller, cutting out a route through a mountain in preparation for a new railway bridge. I was lucky to get this opportunity, but after a while people began to tell me that working underground might affect my health.

I was a strong young lad at the time, but the truth dawned when I saw this workmate – an old boy who had been in the mines all his life – coughing as if his lungs would burst.

I thought this could happen to me but the money was good and I stayed in the job until the outbreak of the war in 1939. Then they wanted people to work at aerodromes up and down the country, and I was able to pack up the bridge job and breathe the fresh air at last. I was very pleased to end that chapter in my life.

B

Back on the cricket front, I was becoming known to people farther afield in first grade cricket which is our Saturday afternoon cricket in Australia. I was asked to go for a trial with Northern Districts at Hornsby and I did so well that I promptly won my first team place.

TWO

Hurricane at Petersham

I took over as a medium pace seamer in an emergency at Northern Districts and have regretted the move ever since.

Northern Districts asked me to take on the job when their fast bowler, Frank Gilmor, broke down. I couldn't resist the challenge. I did fairly well, but I reckon I could have been an even greater success if I had persevered with my leg spinners in those early days.

Don't get me wrong. I have enjoyed myself as a paceman, but let's face it – seamers are ten-a-penny. A leg spinner is worth his weight in gold.

I went from strength to strength at Northern Districts, and in the 1942–43 season I established a new batting aggregate of 1,026. This beat the record set up the previous season by Les Fallowfield, and it still stands today.

I wasn't finished that summer, either. I moved on to Petersham where I became the first player to score more than 1,000 runs in two consecutive seasons. While at Petersham I assured myself a place in cricket history by hitting 230 off the Wranwick bowlers. The local newspaper compared it with Victor Trumper's hurricane record of 335. The old bat certainly sang a sweet tune as I hit 12 sixes and 21 fours.

After scoring these runs – the first 100 took only 59 minutes –

19

I went on to bowl and grabbed six for 52, all in the same afternoon!

Mention of Victor Trumper reminds me that I once played against his son. Young Vic was no great shakes as a batsman, but he was an outstanding fast bowler for New South Wales. He was a big, upstanding lad, about six feet tall. I played against him very early in my career and I was so small they wouldn't let me bat in the first innings. He's much too fast, they said.

They relented in the second knock and put me down at No. 7 or 8. I was wearing sandshoes and young Vic bowled one which hit me right on top of my foot. It split a toe right down the middle and there was enough blood to make a dozen black puddings. Still, I was none the worse for the adventure. In fact, it seemed to do me good. I grew up into a real sapling. I seemed to sprout overnight – and my dear grandmother said it was costing a fortune to keep me in clothes.

In my first season at Petersham, war savings certificates were awarded to players scoring the fastest 100 and the fastest fifties before and after Christmas. I scored the fastest 100 and won a £75 certificate.

About this time I was building myself up physically by working as a blacksmith's striker and boilermaker's assistant at the Everly Workshops, a big repair depot for railway stock, at Sydney. I was very fit and I can recall turning up for a game after a night shift and batting and bowling for three and a half hours one Saturday afternoon.

Sydney cricket had a top-class line-up in the mid-forties. Don Bradman had moved to South Australia, but the stars included Ken Grieves, who later captained Lancashire, Sid Barnes, Arthur Morris, Lindsay Hassett and Colin McCool (my predecessor with Somerset). Keith Miller was still in the Services, but Ray Lindwall was right on top and young Ronnie Hamence, who later played for South Australia, was the talk of the town. Bradman himself reckoned Hamence had a great future as a batsman.

The New South Wales selectors came to watch my duel with left-hander Ernie Toshack on a vicious pitch at Marrickville. This was an innings I recall with particular pride. The pitch had been flooded overnight and Toshack had the ball playing tricks from the first over. I fortified myself with a luncheon snack of oysters, brought over specially from Brooklyn, but I really had to get my head down to master Ernie and score the 100 which clinched my selection for New South Wales against the Services. This was my reply to those critics who had suggested that I was nothing more than a crude slogger. I continued the good work with a stand of 127 with Sid Barnes in the State game and one writer likened me to that great Yorkshire left-hander, Maurice Leyland, which was praise indeed.

I was carried off with a leg injury in the next game against South Australia but not before I hit 111 in a 251-run spree with Barnes who again shared the partnership. Bill ('Tiger') O'Reilly, the pre-war Aussie Test bowler, was a team-mate in this match and he demoralised the South Australians while returning figures of four for 15. I reckon 'Tiger' must have taken nearly 1,000 wickets with St. George's and North Sydney in first grade cricket and yet I seemed to have the knack of drawing his claws.

O'Reilly was a great Australian champion and I always deferred to his wisdom. He once told me: 'When you are batting or bowling you should always regard the man at the other end as your worst enemy!'

I took 'Tiger' at his word in one game against St. George's . . . and carted him all over the field as I rattled up another 100! I was thrilled that I had been able to master 'Tiger' when so many had failed. As a matter of fact, only twice in six seasons did I fail to score more than 50 against O'Reilly.

My first big disappointment came in 1946 when I was passed over for the Australian tour of New Zealand. I had done well in State cricket and was so confident of selection that I had packed my gear. Bradman came to watch me in one State game and told me that I was a near-certainty for the New Zealand tour. The Don's encouragement seemed to merit the go-ahead and I went out and bought myself a dozen new shirts for the trip.

I was really buoyed up at the prospect of an Australian cap but I was jolted out of my daydreams when the team was announced. The newspaper headlines screamed: 'Alley

tragedy' – and a lot of people thought I had been killed or
had committed suicide. They didn't realise what was going on
until it was pointed out that I had missed selection for New
Zealand.

Some time passed before I could rouse myself to unpack my
tour bag and then it was only to hand over those new shirts to
a chap who said he was a member of the tour party. I hope
they brought him luck – but I couldn't have cared less. The
shirts were an awful reminder that the selectors had decided to
leave me behind. I was heartbroken at the time, but looking
back I realise that the selectors had picked a very strong side.
The tour party included Barnes (New South Wales), Billy
Brown (Queensland), Bruce Dooland (South Australia), Ian
Johnson (Victoria), Lindsay Hassett (Victoria), Ronnie
Hamence (South Australia), Ray Lindwall (New South Wales),
Bill O'Reilly (New South Wales) and Ernie Toshack (New
South Wales).

I think Hamence was preferred to me for the New
Zealand tour. Ronnie never achieved my batting averages, but
he was a good player on Australian wickets. Unfortunately, he
couldn't find his touch when he came to England in 1948,
though with such a formidable batting order he often had to
sacrifice his wicket in the chase for runs.

I was delighted but scared when New South Wales selected
me for the game against Wally Hammond's M.C.C. team in
the 1946–47 season. The late Stan McCabe sympathised with
me on the morning of the match. 'I suppose you are very
nervous,' he said. 'Don't worry. I was nervous, too, when I
used to play against these fellows.'

An off-the-record conversation piece between the match
commentators, Arthur Gilligan and Alan McGillvray provided
an amusing interlude. Arthur and Alan had just completed a
broadcast and were chatting away, oblivious of the fact that
the 'mike' hadn't been switched off.

I was batting at the time and I played a ridiculous shot at
Doug Wright, the Kent and England leg spin and googly bowler.
Arthur exclaimed: 'Where does this chap come from – right
up the country? It looked as if he had a shovel in his hand

when he played that shot.' Arthur's comment went out on all networks and old 'Shovel Alley' had to put up with a heap of leg-pulling from friends who heard the broadcast!

During that match I thumped a half-volley from Doug . . . and I can still see John Ikin's eyes as I played the shot. He was fielding really close and the ball went through his hands and struck the offside fence just as he dived to make contact with the ground. If the ball had hit John in the face, it would most likely have killed him.

I overheard Denis Compton, who was fielding on the other side of the wicket, remark to Wally Hammond: 'Skipper, do you mind if I step back a bit?'

After this incident MCC dispensed with their close ring of fieldsmen. They could see I was an aggressive sort of player and they reverted to a more orthodox field.

Bowling at the other end was that great fast-medium bowler Alec Bedser, who used to make a habit of trapping Arthur Morris round his legs. Alec had Bill Edrich at leg slip, and he pitched his first ball perfectly on my leg stump. I managed to steer it between Edrich and wicket-keeper Paul Gibb and it went to the fence for four.

Hammond immediately walked up to Bedser and had a quiet chat with him. Alec did not bowl another ball at my leg stump for the rest of the innings. They must have thought it was a useless tactic. I finished with 40-odd not out and was very pleased to do so well in my first game against the English team.

THREE

K.O. in the nets

A cricket K.O. put an end to my hopes of becoming Australia's welterweight boxing champion. In fact, it nearly put an end to everything . . . including my move to England.

I was in the nets before a match against South Australia at Adelaide when Jock Livingston, who was batting in an adjoining net, played a fierce hook shot just as I was about to pick up another ball. The ball came through a weak section of the netting, hit me on the left hand side of the jaw and poleaxed me. I never moved, didn't flinch a muscle and they whipped me off to hospital. I didn't know a thing for about sixteen hours and Ken Grieves, who was a clubmate of mine at Petersham, said afterwards that he thought I was a goner.

I was so concussed they couldn't operate until I recovered from the shock of the blow. Then they carried out a big operation on the side of my jaw. When I came round from the anaesthetic I was swathed in bandages and a lot of people said I actually looked better in the mask, with only my eyes peeping through!

Seriously, it was a massive reconstruction job – they had to insert about sixty stitches – and the surgeons told me that if the ball had hit me higher up I wouldn't have survived. My face literally just caved in – it felt like a piece of timber snapping – but grace be to God, I've never had any soreness, headaches or lack of vision since the accident. Everyone was frantic with worry. Frankly, I don't think they thought I would come out of it alive.

I went back to Sydney to convalesce and I was still anxious to continue my boxing career, particularly as I had planned some fights in England. I told the specialist of my hopes. He gave me a thorough examination, and warned me that I would be mad to take up boxing again after being so close to death. He said another injury to my face might be fatal.

I had gone to school with Vic Patrick, who later became lightweight champion of Australia. Vic, Ian Cross, the international cyclist, George Cook, who competed for the world professional single sculls title, and I were great pals back in Hawkesbury River. We must have spent hours dreaming of becoming sporting champions and it is marvellous to think that we made the grade in our chosen sports.

I used to spar with Vic and eventually fought a six-rounder which led to my brief career in the ring. I had around twenty-seven bouts and won them all, but I still took some nasty beltings. You couldn't really say who felt worse – the winner or the loser. I know I always had a hangover next morning and I used to shudder when I looked in the shaving-mirror and saw what the other chap had done to my face.

Somewhere back in Sydney, in a little back-street where they don't take kindly to sightseers, there's a dimly-lit alleyway leading from a dance hall where I used to earn £2 a night as a bouncer.

I got the bouncer's job from Ken Grieves, who was playing under me at Petersham. 'Have a go, Bill,' he urged. 'Nothing to it; never have any trouble.'

I should have smelt a rat. On the first night alone I chucked out three drunks. By then Ken was on his way to the Lancashire League – no doubt laughing all the way.

The drill was to pull aside these fellows if you thought they had too much to drink. You would tell the drunk to have a couple of cups of black coffee and come back in half-an-hour if he was sober. If you were lucky, he didn't come back. If he did return, still smelling of alcohol, then you knew you'd picked the wrong chap.

A fight would then be arranged to take place after the dance. It was never a free-for-all brawl. We each had our own second just to see fair play, and we used to scrap in a cul-de-sac at the back of the dance-hall. The first man down was the loser; there was never any question of anyone putting the boot in. We were as civilised as it was possible to be in the circumstances.

As an aspiring welterweight I could handle most of these jokers easily. But there was this Scotsman. I can see him now, a ginger-haired wild man, lurching up to the ballroom. I used to place myself in a position of advantage at the top of the stairs and ram a right into his drunken face. Then I'd left hook him and knock him sideways, but he'd still come barging in and most likely put me down on my backside.

We would fight until we could hardly stand up and this bloke would say: 'I'll see you next week.' So help me, we slugged it out for nine weeks solid until the blood must have flowed down into the harbour.

I'll never forget my astonishment when I went back to Australia after some years in England. I looked in at the dance hall and who should be the chucker-out but my old adversary, the ginger-haired Scot. The management had taken my advice after I'd told them: 'If there is one fellow you want to sign on, rather than have him kill us, it's that bloody Scotsman. He'll be able to knock the others down the road.'

At this reunion we squared up again and he asked: 'Are we going to finish this brawl of ours?' He was on the top step this time. I declined the offer. Instead, we went into the dance hall and had a milk shake apiece. We finished the best of friends. He wasn't a bad scrapper, either.

FOUR

Too old for Australia

Every cricketer's dream is to represent his country – and I was no exception. One of the biggest disappointments of my career was that I missed the Kangaroo on my old cap.

The Aussie selectors reckoned I was too old for Test cricket at thirty but, looking back over all those years, I think perhaps it was a blessing in disguise that I failed to book my tour ticket to England with Don Bradman's great team in 1948. That trip could so easily have been my swan-song. After all, I was getting up in years and who knows what might have happened if I had gone back to Australia after the tour. At all events, I wouldn't have stayed so long in the game.

In those days there was no such thing as getting a good job because of your fame as a cricketer. Arthur Morris was working as a civil servant when he was picked for the 1948 tour. His employers knew that he would be away in England for four or five months and they asked Arthur what he planned to do when he returned home. He naturally told them he planned to play as much cricket as possible. Arthur was given a fortnight's notice. And here was a chap who turned out to be one of Australia's best openers!

My future was really decided by a series of personal tragedies. I ran into a shocking bad patch in 1945. Within the space of six months my first wife died in childbirth and my mother and mother-in-law also died. Since then I've heard people grumble about their problems. They might have broken a cup or something and they say: 'Oh, I have got everything on my shoulders.'

I have thought, if you had as much on your shoulders as I had, you *would* have something to worry about. But I've kept all this to myself. I was left with a young nipper, Ken, and it was a hell of a decision to leave him and make a fresh start in Lancashire League cricket in England in 1948.

Ken was only two years old at the time, but I had some wonderful support from my wife's sister and husband. They said: 'Right, if you have made up your mind to go to England and play professional cricket, we will look after Ken.'

After five years I went back with Betty, my second wife, and her family to bring Ken to England. That was one of the most nervous moments of my life. I wondered: 'How is he going to greet me?'

I needn't have worried. Ken jumped into my arms when we arrived and never left my side all the time we were there. This was a tremendous moment for me – and I shall always be grateful to my sister-in-law and her husband. They had loved Ken, treated him as one of their own, but had always told him that his father was in England and I would be coming back to collect him.

Back in Lancashire the kids were fascinated by Ken's Australian twang. They used to follow him home from school and rile him and get him to talk. Nine times out of ten you would hear a squeal and he would have one of these kids on the cobblestones, pumping the hell out of him.

I used to tell him they have their own language in Lancashire, just as he talked Australian. All of a sudden Ken completely changed his accent and started speaking broader than any Lancastrian!

Bill O'Reilly was the inspiration behind my decision to come to England. 'You'll set them alight.' he said when I dithered about accepting a contract from Colne, the Lancashire League club.

Stan McCabe opposed the move. He tried to persuade me

to stay and realise my ambition to play for Australia. In the end, I accepted O'Reilly's advice – and I can't say I have ever really regretted the move, much as I would have loved that kangaroo on my cap.

The journey to England certainly paid off for me, cobbers. I reckon I've got more out of cricket than anyone who has played the game. I've had seven or eight trips abroad and been to every cricketing country in the world, bar the West Indies. And, even more important to me, I've never played second or third class cricket in my life.

The exodus of young Australian cricketers after the war – more than half a potential Test team left to try their luck in England in the late 1940's and early 1950's – was a bombshell for the Australian administrators.

The Lancashire League clubs had their agents in Sydney. They used to visit the Grade matches and they were on handsome bonuses if they could attract the better players to England.

Before I went to Colne I had an offer from Rawtenstall. We went through all the negotiations, bar actually signing the contract. Then the agent told me that Rawtenstall stipulated their pro. must be a single man. Rawtenstall wanted the player to stay at a local hotel. And when I told them I was married to an Australian girl, this upset the applecart because they only had reservations for a single man.

The hotel was right next to the ground and the Rawtenstall opening batsman, George Hoyle, owned the place. Ray Lindwall went over later and stayed at the Wellsprings Hotel. He was such a big attraction that the hotel was bursting at the seams with customers every night.

Keith Miller and Bob Cristofani, who played with the Australian Services team in the Victory Tests in 1945, were both wanted by Rawtenstall.

Rawtenstall cabled me, asking if I could recommend another player, and I contacted my Petersham team-mate, Ken Grieves. Now Ken was only a young lad – he'd never left his mother's side – and he was worried about travelling 13,000 miles to the other side of the world to play cricket.

I told Ken: 'There is no need to be worried. Go across and see the world. You'll be all right.'

Ken bowled only a little for Petersham and he said that Rawtenstall had asked him for his bowling figures. I replied: 'What difference does it make? They won't contact anybody about them – put down 6–40 or 8–25.'

Well, Ken eventually came across to England and he had no problems as a bowler. He started to bowl them out and did as well with the ball as with the bat! And he went on to captain Lancashire. I suppose you could say that if he had gone to Rawtenstall as an amateur, he would have been just a normal player. But the difference was he had the name of pro. on his head and everyone was afraid of him.

Ken made his home in England and he married a girl from Rawtenstall, the same part of Lancashire as my second wife, Betty, comes from.

The offer from Colne came soon after the family bereavements and the injury in the nets at Adelaide. This time I didn't give them a chance to change their minds. I thought I couldn't be more unlucky in England.

The Lancashire League contracts started to flow into Australia and I was one of several Aussies who made the grade in England. Cecil Pepper, George Tribe, Ken Grieves, Jock Livingston, who was a brilliant 'keeper and batsman, and Bruce Dooland all left when they were on the point of being selected for Australia.

The Australian Cricket Board of Control never forgave us for flying off to England. When I went back to Australia with Betty and her father and mother there was no welcome on the mat. You'll have to pay, they told us at the Sydney Cricket Ground. The chap on the gate said: 'I daren't let you in. You'll have to show a ticket.'

There was no question, either, of us playing for New South Wales. The bitterness was so deep that the State selectors wouldn't entertain the idea of us as guest players. The other states were more lenient and Bruce Dooland and George Tribe played in a few games when they returned to Australia.

The selectors' attitude seemed harsh after all those years. All right, so we had turned our back on Australia as youngsters, but it is ironical to think that our home country has been pleased to accept chaps like Wes Hall and Tony Lock as coaches and players. Just fancy, outsiders going out to teach Australians how to play cricket. How times change!

Certainly, it didn't give me any pleasure to learn of the decline of Australian cricket after 1948. I remember playing in a Bank-holiday match at Gordon, Jack Pettiford's old club, against Siddie Barnes when I returned to Australia in the mid-fifties. The game started at 11 or 11.30, an all-day match, and I don't suppose there were more than fifty people on the ground. It was a depressing experience to listen to the echo of bat on ball in a near empty ground.

FIVE

'They'll diddle you out'

I played my first game in England in a snowstorm and failed to heed the warning of a local school-teacher.

He had watched me batting in the nets for a week after my arrival in Colne in 1948 and, after one practice session, he drew me on one side and said: 'They won't get you out in the League – you'll get a lot of runs. But take a tip from me – they'll diddle you out.'

On my début day the skies were grey and the crowd were muffled up in their overcoats. And those big snowflakes were really something out of this world for me, a newcomer from the sunshine of Australia.

One of Colne's opponents was Arthur Booth, the Yorkshire left-arm bowler and I was just getting in the mood, having taken 13 runs off Arthur, when an off-spinner by the name of John Ingham, came on to bowl at the other end.

The first ball this amateur tweaker threw up pitched outside my leg stump and I never attempted to play it. Next minute I was flabbergasted to hear a hell of a rattle. In those days team-mates and opponents used to call you 'pro.'. The wicket-keeper just said to me: 'You're out bowled, pro.'

I replied: 'You must be bloody joking.' Well, I turned round and he was right. The three stumps were in a sorry mess. I still

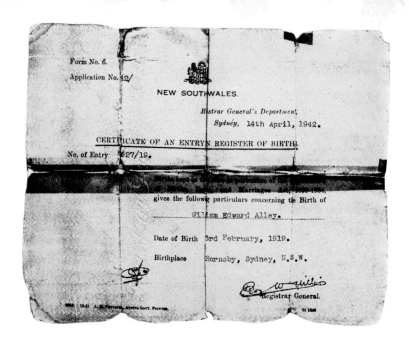

Form No. 6.

Application No. 42/

NEW SOUTH WALES.

Registrar General's Department,
Sydney, 14th April, 1942.

CERTIFICATE OF AN ENTRY IN REGISTER OF BIRTH.

No. of Entry 627/19.

gives the following particulars concerning the Birth of

William Edward Alley.

Date of Birth   3rd February, 1919.

Birthplace   Hornsby, Sydney, N.S.W.

Registrar General.

Above: I have enjoyed the fun of being called W.G.'s brother and the grand-daddy of county cricket, but I have never lied about my age. The truth is that I have never revealed it. Other people have insisted that they had proof that I had an old age pension book in my hip pocket. Here, now, is my proof. Just like me it's a bit tattered and torn, with a few creases . . . but William Edward Alley, is, as you can now see, just a babe . . . *Below:* The start of the Incredible Innings. The author, third from right back row, with Poideven-Gray Shield team in New South Wales

Deep in thought with Ernie Crossen before opening in a friendly match in New South Wales

With the New South Wales side in 1946. *Back row:* W. Donaldson, W. Beath, K. Grieves, J. Pettiford, R. Lindwall and myself. *Front row:* K. Carmody, A. Morris, S. Barnes (capt.), A. Alterator (Manager), F. Saggers, E. Toshack and G. Powell

couldn't believe it – and had to be told to go by the umpire. He didn't give me out in a nice manner either. 'That's out!' he snapped, and pointed sternly to the pavilion, as if to say 'get moving . . . or else'.

My old friend, the schoolmaster came up to me after the match and said: 'I told you they wouldn't get you out. They diddled you out!' I got my revenge with a hundred against Rawtenstall the following Saturday.

This was a good lesson. The ball must have spun sixteen inches in the mud. I never failed again to cover my wicket, and it put me in good form for the cricket that followed.

The locals had given me a marvellous welcome when I arrived from Australia. This place, Colne – it's on the Lancashire–Yorkshire border – is a grand little town. But I had a shock when I went to look at their ground. I thought to myself, what sort of a pitch is this? Remember I'd been used to playing on a Test ground at Sydney in Australia.

There was only a week to go before the start of the season and I couldn't see any sign of a wicket out there in the middle. Colne must have noticed my surprise and they told me: 'Don't worry, Bill. There'll be a wicket on the day. It only takes a week to make one.'

We went from strength to strength in my first season at Colne and finished second in the table, missing the title by five runs in the last match.

They gave me the tag of 'Colne's Atlas' in the Lancashire League, and I suppose I earned it playing in the great company of professionals which included Everton Weekes at Bacup, Cecil Pepper at Burnley, Bruce Dooland at East Lancashire and my old mate, Ken Grieves, at Rawtenstall.

I topped the batting averages with 1,151 runs in my first season at Colne, and I was only the seventh batsman in the league's history to score over 1,000 in one season.

You could say I earned my keep in that first season. I hit three 100's and managed over 50 in thirteen innings. They couldn't fault me as a bowler, either. I grabbed 86 wickets at just over 12 runs apiece and I am sure I would have done the double but for a spot of back trouble late in the season.

In those palmy days they described League cricket as the

C

'street of adventure literally paved with gold' and the knowledgeable Lancashire folk always showed their appreciation of keen and lively cricket. In my first season at Colne I collected over £300 from the fans. They gave me a £32 collection when I lashed thirty boundaries in an innings of 147 against Nelson.

The crowds warmed to big hitters like myself, but they also understood that it was sometimes necessary to build an innings. They'd help you by their appreciation. If you went in and missed your 50 by three or four runs they would still cheer you to the echo. They knew their cricket and the bobs and the tanners would roll into the boxes.

Playing in the Lancashire League improved my technique and I soon learned that I couldn't throw my bat at the ball with a top-class professional bowler operating at one end all the time.

The professional worked with the groundsman in the preparation of wickets required against particular opposition. If you were playing against a spinner, you'd water the ground until the grass started to sprout up. On the other hand, if you were up against a first-class seamer, you would be down there chewing the bloody grass with your false teeth.

We failed by five runs to clinch the Lancashire League title in a cliffhanger at Ramsbottom on the last Saturday of the 1948 season. Ramsbottom set us a target of 166 in around two hours and we went hell for leather for the runs. We lost four wickets for 37 and needed to score at the rate of two runs a minute in the last hour.

The light was shocking, but two of the lads, Schofield and Bradshaw, banged away and the scoreboard raced round until we were only 27 short with 12 minutes left.

Schofield was bowled for 20 and Bradshaw hit a boundary for his 50 before he holed out at square-leg trying for the runs which would have put us level. And that was that. There wasn't time for our last man, Hyndman Snell, to get out to the middle.

We still might have beaten Ramsbottom if the game hadn't started thirteen minutes late. There was a mix-up over the wicket. When the two skippers, Ellis Dickinson and Bill Whitworth, went out to toss they found the match wicket wasn't fit for play. So the groundsman had to mark out another strip before we could get started.

I seem to remember that this game produced an unusual record. There was a very long boundary on one side of the Ramsbottom ground and there were five fours, all run, in the two innings.

To add to our frustration we heard that Rishton had won the title after a desperately close match with Rawtenstall.

We were disappointed at just failing to bring the title to Colne, but we did the next best thing by winning the Worsley Cup for the first time in twenty-four years. This was another thriller at Horsfield and we just scraped home by two wickets against East Lancashire. We were six behind when the eighth wicket fell and Ellis Dickinson, who was also our wicket-keeper, made the winning hit.

At Colne I soon learned that the Lancastrians were wise in the ways of cricket. They wanted to see the ball hit and they hated you if you got out cheaply. If you made a hundred, however, you could walk down the street on Monday morning and kick the bishop up the backside!

If you failed and lost the match, they would blame you and nobody else. You were the pro., the organiser of the attack and the spectators were paying you to win games.

The professional learned to be tolerant and philosophical about the outcricket of the ordinary club player. The amateur boys were 100-per-cent behind you, but they had to work five days a week to earn their living and you couldn't talk to them in the way you would speak to a county player.

If you did lose your temper at a dropped catch, they would say: 'Well, who do you think we are? We are not professionals.'

They expected the professional to deliver the goods. If the team scored 200, the pro was expected to contribute a score of between 110 and 130. You opened the bowling, even if you were a spinner, and nine times out of ten you bowled right through an innings.

The responsibility was considerable, but I didn't fail Colne very often. In three seasons I scored half as many centuries as the rest of the players who had turned out for the club.

A glance at my scrapbook, kept by my wife, reveals the following list of my performances: *1948:* 102 n.o. v Rawtenstall; 147 v Nelson; 143 n.o. v Church. *1949:* 101 n.o. v Burnley; 143 n.o. v Nelson; 102 n.o. v East Lancashire; 132 n.o. v Church. *1950:* 100 n.o. v East Lancashire; 142 v Nelson; 120 n.o. v Enfield. *1951:* 153 v Bacup; 105 n.o. v Enfield; 158 n.o. v Bacup; 106 n.o. v Accrington.

In addition, I scored an unbeaten 101 against Nelson in the Express Cup and 142 against Church in the Worsley Cup competition in the 1948 season.

We lost only three games in the 1948 season. Rennie Mitchell was our leading amateur with a run tally of 446. I was very fortunate in having such an unselfish player as Rennie to keep an end going. As a bowler, too, I couldn't have had a better ally than that old warhorse Hyndman Snell, who followed me in the averages with 54 wickets.

Church and Nelson were my favourite victims as a batsman. I expect they wished many times that I had never left Australia. I always seemed to be able to master the Church left-armer Fred Hartley, who had a magnificent record in the league.

I remember one game in which I gave Fred a real caning. After four overs I could sense that he was in danger of being taken off. So I went all canny. I fumbled and prodded my way through his next over. Each ball seemed likely to take wicket. I shouted in acknowledgement: 'Well bowled, Fred.' The Church skipper fell for it. Fred was kept on – and I continued where I left off.

I think it was in this game against Fred that I jumped from 80 to a 100 with four shots – 4, 6, 4, 6. Yes, I enjoyed myself against Church. In three innings against them I scored 417 runs for once out.

Poor old Nelson came in for a bit of stick, too. I expect they'll always remember the day in June, 1949, when they dropped me before I had scored and allowed me to knock up 143.

Colne had lost two wickets for four runs when I came in to bat. It ought to have been four for three. I was beaten twice in my first two balls and off the third I snicked a catch straight into the wicket-keeper's gloves. I think he was actually appealing for a catch when the ball slipped from his grasp and on to the ground.

I didn't provide them with another chance and gave a repeat performance in topping the 140 mark at their expense for the second time in two seasons. We bowled out Nelson for 109 and I took six for 29 to round off a pleasant afternoon's cricket.

The big money lure of the Lancashire League pulled in seven overseas stars for the 1949 season. There were two world record-breakers in the Indian, Vijay Hazare (Rawtenstall), who had shared a Test record stand of 577 with Gul Mahomed for Baroda against Holkar in 1946–47, and that brilliant West Indian, Everton Weekes (Bacup), who scored five Test hundreds on the trot between 1947 and 1949.

A reported £10,000 was being shared among the fourteen professionals in 1949 and it was reckoned that players were on £600–£1,000 for the season, plus collections. In a needle game or a Bank-holiday match a pro. could net between £30 and £50 and there was no income tax to pay on this little bonus.

The season started with a bang. Rishton's Australian pro., Fred Freer, took all 10 wickets for 27 runs against Haslingden, but still finished on the losing side. Hazare hit 50 against East Lancashire and Everton Weekes won his duel with Burnley's new pro., Cecil Pepper. He had the nerve to bowl out big Cec. for six. I weighed in with 6–55 which helped put out Church for 104.

East Lancashire, with Aussie leg-spinner, Bruce Dooland, were the team of the season and nobody had a hope of catching them as they raced past the title post.

Although Colne finished well down the table we beat East Lancashire once and were only 28 short of victory with eight wickets left in the return game against Bruce's lads at Colne.

I used to joke to Bruce: 'I could pick your bloody googlie out in a cellar on a dark night' – and I was happy to put this into practice in our famous victory over East Lancashire that season.

That game at Blackburn was a real treat for the crowd. 374 runs were scored in less than five hours. East Lancashire gave us a target of 186. I hadn't done much with the ball and so I had to earn my pay with the bat.

We lost 4 wickets for 64 before Ken Parrington joined me in a fifth wicket stand. We put on 76 and I whacked five fours off successive balls. I went on to score 84 before Dooland hung on to a skier at mid-on. But he was too late to prevent us from clinching a two-wicket win with just four minutes to spare.

Burnley gave us a hammering at Turf Moor that season. Cecil Pepper and Riley put on a 100 for the first wicket and they rattled up 209 for four wickets down. We didn't give up without a fight and I gave them a taste of their own medicine with a quick-fire 100 in 85 minutes.

We finished with 148 but the rest of the Colne lads had an off-day. Eight batsmen could muster only 11 runs between them.

I set up a Lancashire League record when I scored 90 not out against Enfield, and became the only batsman to score 1,000 runs in successive seasons. I bettered my 1948 run tally with 1,278 (average: 63.90) and was third in the league averages behind Weekes and Hazare, who topped both the batting and bowling lists.

Everton established a Bacup club batting record when he passed the previous best total of 1,193 with an unbeaten 195 against Enfield. This was the biggest innings ever recorded in the league and my great rival went on to score 1,470 runs that season.

Weekes beat me by 70 runs to the 1,000 in 1949, and he was always a little ahead of me in our duels each season. The local papers used to write about our rivalry each week and it was always a talking point as to which of us would reach the 1,000 first. But in my own mind I always knew who was going to do it. I did not put myself in Everton's class, although he never scored many more runs than me. He was a *great* player and he would score a classic 140, hitting his fours on the carpet while I was clouting them over the fence for six with my more aggressive style.

Ray Lindwall, who came over to England after I had left Colne to join Blackpool in the Northern League, followed in the footsteps of the legendary Learie Constantine at Nelson. A crowd of nearly 8,000 people saw Lindwall play in his first game against Church.

The reputation of a bowler who had knocked down the castles of Len Hutton and Denis Compton rocketed the Nelson membership to a record 1,600. But Ray didn't have a happy start with Nelson. He found the Lancashire League was no respecter of reputations, but it must be said in his defence that he didn't have the support of the best close fieldsmen in the world as he had back home.

Naturally, it wasn't fair to expect Saturday afternoon amateurs to take blinding catches off the meat of the bat in the style of Benaud or Davidson. Ray soon realised that it was his job to knock the stumps out of the ground.

Breezy Blackpool always seemed to bring the best out of me even before I went to live there and play for the Northern League club in 1953.

I remember one match in which I turned out for Fred Freer's Australian XI against the Seasiders in the 1949 season. We were set a target of 190 in 80 minutes – a big total even by league standards – and I took the Blackpool bowling by the scruff of the neck. I really cut loose and hit the first of my nine sixes off the second ball I received. My first 50 was scored in half-an-hour; I scorched to a 100 out of 130 in 54 minutes; and hit the match-winning six to reach 150 in 70 minutes. Even Cecil Pepper, who was no slouch as a hitter, gasped as he watched from the other end. I think Cec. dawdled to about 30 in our second wicket stand.

As I say, I didn't mind Blackpool – Stanley Park seemed to suit my style. I scored 304 in three innings there that week.

That year, 1949, was a great one for me in more ways than cricket. It also marked my engagement to a Rawtenstall telephone girl, Betty Cortman, to whom I had said 'hello' at a dance soon after my arrival in England the previous year. We announced our engagement to coincide with the silver wedding of Betty's parents, Mr and Mrs Jack Cortman. Betty and I were married at St Paul's Church, Constable Lee, on September 14 and my best man was my old Aussie mate, Jack Pettiford.

We had time only for a honeymoon at Scarborough before I left with an all-professional Commonwealth side to tour India, Pakistan and Ceylon.

SIX

How's that for style?

The late George Duckworth, the great England and Lancashire wicket-keeper, who managed Commonwealth teams on several tours to India, labelled me a slogger when we played at Poona.

He was also writing reports on the tour for an English newspaper and he nettled me when he said I was a crude basher, without style. I saw the copy before he sent it off and I thought to myself: 'I'll make George eat his words.' I was just over 100 not out that night and we didn't get back from a cocktail party until nearly four the next morning. I snatched a few hours' sleep and when I got up I thought 'Right, you red rascal, George. Now I'll show you what a straight bat is.'

The day was typically steamy with the temperature in the 90's – and I went on to score another 100. But this time I played it strictly by the book. I batted for four hours and I'd be lying if I said I got more than five fours in that ton! After the innings I threw my bat in the corner and had a shower. George, who was scoring, came into the dressing-room after he had totted up the runs.

He looked mighty pleased with himself and said: 'We've had a good day, boys.' I cheered and said: 'I think I've had a bloody good day, too. Now there's something to put in your paper. And if you like you can add, "Alley made a bloody fool of me and played the innings of his life. He never lifted the ball off the ground and played straight to every ball".' George grinned sheepishly, but didn't say anything more. Instead, he got up and walked out of the room!

Jock Livingston skippered the all-professional side which toured India, Pakistan and Ceylon that winter. The tour was arranged in place of the MCC trip, which had been cancelled and I think we probably had a better side than England could have mustered at that time.

There were nine Australians in the party: Fred Freer (Rishton), George Tribe (Milnrow), Cecil Pepper (Burnley), Jack Pettiford (Nelson), fast bowlers Des Fitzmaurice (Ashton) and Harry Lambert (Ramsbottom), and Wally Langdon, who joined us from Western Australia, in addition to Jock and myself.

The team also included the great Frank Worrell and fellow West Indian, J. K. Holt, as well as Winston Place, George Pope and Norman Oldfield, all of whom had played for England, and Ray Smith, that very useful all-rounder from Essex.

Worrell gave us a good start with a 100 in the first match against the Indian Universities at Bombay and we then flew by specially chartered plane to Ahmedabad for a game on matting against Western India, captained by Vijay Hazare.

Pope, Pepper and Tribe were in deadly form as we put out Western India twice in one day to win by an innings. In the next match at Indore, Cec. got the first hat-trick of the tour when we bundled out the Holkar XI for 86.

Wally Langdon hit 66 out of 190, but the local side gave us a real fright by piling up 300 in the second innings. Gaekwad, who was later selected for India in the first unofficial Test at Delhi, was the local hero when he bagged five wickets in our first innings.

He very nearly won the match, too, as we chased a target of 190 in the second innings. He took another six wickets and twice beat our last man, George Pope with sizzling deliveries before George made the winning hit.

I think it was while we were staying in Bombay that I first came to grips with a big parrot which had a sharp beak and an unfriendly nature. We had been up late that night, drinking whisky and eating lobsters. It got to about half-past two in the morning and Frankie Worrell and Jock Livingston were trying their hardest to persuade me to go to bed. I couldn't understand it. I was always ready to burn the midnight oil. But Frankie and Jock kept insisting, 'Bill, it's about time you went to bed as you've a hard day ahead of you.'

We were staying in a big suite – they were like magnificent flats – attached to the Bombay cricket stadium. Eventually I decided I needed my bed and off I trounced. You never use pyjamas in India – they are only there in case of fire – so I was 'starkers' when I jumped into bed, pulling a sheet over me to ward off the mosquitoes and other undesirable intruders.

The next moment there was one hell of a bloody commotion. Feathers flew about and so did I – straight out of bed! As I did so there was this parrot gripping my how's your father!

I couldn't shake the wretched thing off. The more I yelled, the more the ruddy feathers flew all over the shop. All of a sudden, I heard voices and laughter and there were all the bloody team watching me struggle on the floor with the bird. Apparently Jack Pettiford had been to the market that day and bought this green parrot. The lads hit on the plan of pushing the bird into my bed and persuading me to turn in first that night. The blighters . . . It could have done me a very awkward injury!

Poor old Jack Pettiford, who died recently, was involved in another incident shortly after our arrival back at our Bombay headquarters after the first Test. Cecil Pepper, Jack and I were bunking together in this big suite. And about three or four o'clock in the morning we were awakened by a smell of burning. Our room was filled by dense smoke. We were nearly choking to death and all we could see was that Jack's mattress was smouldering. Jack himself was still snoring his head off, unaware of the fire. So we lifted him out of bed before dumping the mattress out of the window. He was so full of booze that we had a hell of a job to wake him up.

The fire had burnt all around his body. Even his wallet and rupees under the pillow were charred. When we tried to rouse Jack he abused us. And then he jumped across into Cec.'s bed and started to snore his bloody head off again.

Jack was a person who used to smoke in bed and he didn't realise that if we hadn't pulled him out we could all have been burnt to death.

We hit our best form in the match against the North Zone at Patiala. Norman Oldfield, Worrell and Ray Smith scored hundreds and I topped 50 in as many minutes with three sixes and five fours. We finished with 613–7 after being sent in to bat. Ray Smith and Jack Pettiford skittled the home side for 168 in the first innings, but we had to be content with a draw.

In the next match, against a Services XI, I knocked up my first century of the tour and shared a fourth wicket stand of 237 with Jock Livingston, who was leg-before one short of his hundred.

Adhikari scored a 100 in the Services' second innings to save an innings defeat, but we had no trouble in winning by 10 wickets.

Vijay Merchant, one of the finest batsmen ever to play for India – he had played against our manager, George Duckworth, in a pre-war Test – skippered India in the first Test at Delhi.

He had a strong team with Hazare, Umrigar, Modi and Phadkar, but their fielding let them down. Livingston and Oldfield put on 226 for the first wicket but they were helped by dropped catches. Oldfield was missed three times, one a dolly by Merchant at mid-off.

I scored 44 before Nayudu rattled my stumps with the last ball of the day. We piled on the agony next morning. Worrell, Freer and Pettiford all got fifties and, apart from the bowling of Nayudu, it was all a bit too easy.

Phadkar and Adhikari gave us trouble with a fifth wicket stand of 161, but Cec. Pepper got among the wickets and India were all out for 291.

Hazare batted brilliantly for 140 in the second innings, but the last five wickets went down for 28 runs. We needed 12 runs for victory and lost Fred Freer in getting them.

We then went on a run spree against the West Zone at Poona. Frankie Worrell and Fred Freer put on 205 in 165 minutes. I was dropped behind the wicket at two before I joined in the fun and added another 100 runs with Frankie.

That was the match in which I got my own back on George

Duckworth with a sedate second 100 to go with a brisk first ton. George Pope helped me to put on another 123 for the seventh wicket.

We finished with 611 and the spectators came out to garland me with flowers when I passed my double century. It seemed an innocent enough celebration. But when the fun was over, I thought I was seeing things. In the next few overs the ball started bouncing about all over the place. I soon discovered why: my barefooted Indian worshippers had concealed tiny pebbles between their toes. During the garland celebrations they had been dropping them on a length at each end of the pitch.

The second Test at Bombay was played at a funereal pace compared with our earlier run-making adventures. This time, we really had to struggle against some tight bowling by Phadkar and Modi. Winston Place batted four hours for 110 and Frankie Worrell weighed in with 78 in a third wicket stand of 188.

The game pulled in one of the biggest crowds ever seen at the Brabourne Stadium. Between 50,000 and 60,000 people squeezed into the ground.

Harry Lambert and Fred Freer tore into the Indian batting with the new ball and India failed by nine runs to save the follow-on. But the second innings was a different story. Merchant and Modi shared a century stand and both just missed their hundreds, while Polly Umrigar, then the bright hope of Indian cricket, scored 63.

They finished with 430 and George Tribe came in for his first real hammering of the tour. His four wickets cost him 154 runs.

India gave us an impossible task in the second innings. We had to score 271 in 110 minutes but I hit a 50 which proved useful batting practice.

George Tribe was back in business again against Pakistan at Lahore. J. K. Holt was a century-maker and George cracked a quick 50 before coaxing the Pakistanis to their doom. At one stage in the Pakistan second innings George took four wickets in five overs without conceding a run. He finished with 5-8, bundling them out for 66. The Pakistan opener Nazar scored 31 and only one other batsman got into double figures. That was certainly a convincing demolition job by George Tribe and we romped home by an innings and 177 runs.

We played the third Test at the beautiful Eden Gardens ground in Calcutta. Hazare was skipper in place of Merchant, who had been injured in the first Test. He was cheered to the echo after scoring an unbeaten 175. I reckon they must have heard the roar on the other side of the Ganges.

India totalled 422, and Worrell, Holt and I could muster only 17 runs between us against Phadkar (3–50) and Chowdbury (4–56). Jock Livingston was our top scorer with 42 and we followed on 232 runs behind. Norman Oldfield came to our rescue with his third Test hundred of the tour and we managed to scrape a draw.

Just to be different Norman got a duck in the fourth Test, played on a matting on red gravel wicket at the industrial town of Kanpur, which was staging its first Test match. Frankie Worrell gave it his blessing with a jewel of a double century.

SEVEN

More records at Colne

George Headley, the 'Black Bradman', who returned to Lancashire League cricket with Bacup in 1950, beat me to the 1,000 by two hours. But I topped the league averages for the second time in three seasons – in another record-breaking year with Colne.

We lost our first match against Ramsbottom by seven wickets and my Indian tour team-mate Harry Lambert took 6–26 as we were bowled out for 91. This game was watched by Ramsbottom's 86-year-old president, Mr Bill Fenwick, who, 50 years before, had taken seven East Lancashire wickets for three runs. East Lancashire were skittled for eight – the lowest total in the history of the league.

Nelson, who seemed to make a habit of missing me before I had scored – they gave me four lives in four innings – came in for another hammering in a local Cup match at Horsfield. I rattled up 101 not out in the Colne total of 150–4 to complete my third century in six appearances against the Seedhill bowlers. My record against Nelson was: 147, 143, 101, 98, 82, 56 – average, 156.

Nelson turned the tables on us in the Worsley Cup derby at Horsfield. Jack Earnshaw, a recruit from the Nelson Sunday League, was almost unplayable. He took seven wickets for 31 and claimed five of our last six wickets for only 15 runs.

Headley, who was the Haslingden pro. in the 1930's, celebrated his return to league cricket with two unbeaten centuries in two days for Bacup. George, who was standing in for Everton Weekes – on Test duty with the West Indies – had an average of 370 after five innings – not bad going for another 50-year-old!

East Lancashire went on a run spree against us at Alexandra Meadows where a big crowd paid £317 in gate money. They hit 206–5 but I put an end to their victory gallop with another 100.

The Bacup locals couldn't believe it when I bowled Headley for 22 in the next game. With George in such good form, they didn't think they would have any trouble in scoring 196 for victory. It looked that way, too, when George cracked me for five fours in quick time. Then I produced a good 'un which knocked over his dolls and Bacup were lucky to scramble a draw.

This was one of seven draws in nine games, but we fought back from a losing position to break the ice with a 22-run win over Ramsbottom. Whitworth hit 53 for Ramsbottom but I took their last three wickets in six balls which gave me figures of 6–69.

Nelson and my old mate, Jack Pettiford, made us pay for their past humiliations with a big win at Nelson. Jack Shea grabbed five wickets and I scored 20 and Norman Ingham 19 out of a total of 60. The rest of the lads were almost forming a queue to get back into the pavilion and our last five wickets fell for 10 runs.

We were back on top in the return game at Horsfield. I passed the 800 mark with my fourth hundred against the Nelson boys, but Pettiford scored 76 and we had to be content with a draw.

Burnley and Cecil Pepper were the big guns in 1950 and they steamrollered us to two defeats in seven days. In the first game at Turf Moor big Cec. bowled magnificently to take 8–32 and earn a collection of £40 10s. – the second highest collection in league history.

Cecil was again on the warpath in the return game at Horsfield on the following Saturday. He and Riley put on 172 for the second wicket and Cec. missed his 100 by only two runs.

Pepper gobbled up our lads with 4–27, and I was left with 44 not out in our total of 73.

Burnley were the league champions and Worsley Cup winners in 1950, but we brought off a surprise when we beat them in the Burnley Express Challenge Cup final. I hit 95 – Cec. Pepper had me caught on the boundary edge – and we totalled 128. This seemed a moderate target for the champions, but I managed to dismiss Pepper for six and we bowled them out for 61.

Fred Hartley, the Church professional, topped the league bowling averages with 84 wickets at an average of 8.19 per wicket. I had a final run tally of 1,131 (average 87) and headed the batting averages.

Bruce Dooland spun us to defeat in the opening match of the 1951 season against East Lancashire at Alexandra Meadows. Bruce captured 6–14 while skittling us for 33 in just over an hour and I was the only Colne batsman to reach double figures.

Then we ran into old Fred Hartley at his brilliant best. He seemed harmless enough at the start and we hit him for 41 while he took only one wicket. *We didn't score another run* as Fred removed our last five Colne batsmen.

Fred was then aged forty-five and I suppose this was all in a day's work for him. I used to give him a bit of stick now and again, but he was a cunning old warhorse. He had twice taken 10 wickets in an innings, once against Rishton in 1947 and against Bacup way back in 1924.

We passed another record milestone at Colne when Ken Parrrington and I put on 221 for the second wicket against Bacup. This beat the previous club record partnership of 185, set up by Schofield and myself against Church in 1949. Ken was unbeaten with 76 and I scored 153 (100 in 75 minutes) to crack the individual batting record of 149 recorded by Herbert Crabtree against Bacup in 1914.

West Indian Test star Clyde Walcott, who had come over to pro. with Enfield, rubbed the smiles off our faces with a great 100 after Norman Ingham and I rattled up 169 for the fourth wicket. Norman hit 90 and I scored another ton out of the Colne total of 221.

The dominance of the overseas pro's. in the Lancashire League was said to be driving the better amateurs into taking

Opening my shoulders in practice at the Petersham Oval, Sydney

Above, left: In a striking mood. This time with blacksmith's hammer during my 'working' days in Sydney. *Above, right:* Taking a break during my years as a car trimmer's assistant at a Sydney railway works . . . *Below:* Sparring session at a Sydney dance hall, keeping fit for my job as a 'bouncer'

pro. jobs in the smaller leagues. People reckoned that the up-and-coming lads were getting the confidence knocked out of them by the Test stars.

I always maintained that the amateurs would get their 50 and 60 wickets in the Lancashire League. They would take these wickets because every batsman played it canny against the pro's. and tried to get his runs off the amateur. By forcing the pace against the amateur boys they got themselves out.

A thumb injury in fielding practice put me out of the game for a month and gave Everton Weekes, back in league action, the field to himself in the chase for the 1,000. At the time of the accident, Everton had scored 465 in seven innings for an average of 93. But I was well in the running with 328 in four innings and an even better average of 109.

Fred Trueman, then a strapping young lad of twenty, came over to pro. for Colne during my absence. Fred got a bit of a roasting from the Burnley batsmen, as I shall relate elsewhere in this book. He started well enough by having Bruce Pairaudeau, the West Indies batsman, caught in the slips off the seventh ball of his first over and then bowled Cocker with a full toss in his next over. He also bowled Ormerod but this was his last success. Thirty-three runs were hit off two overs and the local paper was not impressed by this import from Yorkshire.

They rapped the Colne skipper for his management of the bowling and reported: 'Trueman was kept on far too long.'

We got another hammering from Burnley in the return match and five Colne batsmen failed to score as Cec. Pepper took 6–28 to bundle us out for 74.

EIGHT

Into my third career

Up in Lancashire we soon formed our own Australian team. We sported caps bearing the old kangaroo and contracted to play a series of Sunday matches over a period of three years.

Some of the clubs did not mind their Australian pro's. playing on the Sabbath day, but Colne got very 'sticky' about it. We had arranged Sunday fixtures over a wide area, anything up to a fifty-mile radius of Manchester, and we attracted some colossal gates. The professionals were household names and I reckon there are not many teams which you could select on Sunday afternoons nowadays which would give the crowd better value for money than our bunch of chaps provided.

Those Sunday 'festival' games proved worthwhile for the players, and the clubs we played against made about £150 out of the fixtures.

The Central Lancashire League clubs were only too happy to make money out of Sunday matches. An influential faction, however, were determined that there should never be any Sunday cricket played on Lancashire League grounds. Eventually it came to the point where clubs would not release us to play on Sundays and something had to be done about it.

I had had five happy years at Colne and if they had been

prepared to let me play with the Aussie team, I am certain that everything would have worked out all right.

I hope it doesn't sound too immodest after all this time to say that my style of cricket appealed to the Sunday afternoon spectators and I wanted to cash in on it.

I had had other differences of opinion with Colne about small things. Frank Wilson, their Chairman, who is still a good friend of mine, was tough and insisted on sticking to the letter of all agreements. But he could be kind, too. On one occasion when he knew that, by taking a hard line, he had deprived me of a special match fee, he dug into his own pocket to compensate me.

At the time I was having trouble over the Sunday games I was also trying to get a grouse put before the Committee. One night I waited outside the Committee headquarters to find out if a request I had put forward had been considered. I was supposed to make myself available to coach players three nights a week but they turned up on only two nights and I wanted the extra night off.

I eventually blew my top and the dispute got into the papers. When the fans heard that I might be leaving Colne they organised a public meeting in the Town Hall. Everybody got up and said their piece and although the air was cleared, the general opinion was that I would still quit Colne.

As a matter of fact, I might have gone earlier but no other Lancashire League club could approach me without being liable to pay a fine. If it had been easy to change clubs and stay in the League, I might have gone to Accrington. In fact, I think it was Bill Bradley at Accrington who was partly instrumental in me joining the Blackpool club in 1953. He got in touch with his brother Tom in Blackpool and a meeting was arranged in a local newspaper office to discuss terms prior to joining the Northern League club.

Great care was taken to ensure that no-one knew I was in Blackpool for the talks. They made me a very good offer – and I agreed to sign. Although the standard of cricket was not so high in the Northern League, Blackpool were the premier side and they treated me very well, indeed.

It was inevitable, I suppose, that I would leave Colne because

I had my feathers ruffled too often and being more mellow about things now (I hope!) I am surprised that those tolerant people were prepared to put up with me for so long!

I know I was very angry on the night we celebrated winning the Worsley Cup. I believe in playing cricket as tough as possible because the object is to win. But once the game is over everybody should be treated equally and I could not understand why the East Lancashire team were left out of the celebrations after we had beaten them in the final. I reckoned that we should have all celebrated together and I refused to join in without the East Lancs boys.

I think the root of my trouble at Colne was the underlying uncertainty of everything and the feeling of insecurity. Perhaps if I had been born in Lancashire or had grown up there, I would not have felt the nagging twinge about the future. Nobody, anywhere, could have been kinder to me than the people of Colne. But even then I was an old man playing a young man's game. I was competing for the fruits, which were then very ripe, but no-one could say how long they would last.

And while I felt insecure at times, the cricket committees were also not very certain of themselves. Being good businessmen, they would commit themselves for so much and not a fraction more. I was given verbal assurances about the future, and when I decided to leave Blackpool in 1956 I was fairly certain that I could have continued playing for the club for many years. Blackpool, however, were not prepared to give me more than a year-by-year contract. I was with Blackpool for four years before that time came, and we had a lot of good cricket. I thought I would finish my career in Blackpool, and bought a house and planned it as a permanent home. It was in the same street in which Brian London, the boxer, lived, and just behind singer Josef Locke's place.

Soccer's incredible Peter Pan, Sir Stanley Matthews, became a great buddy of mine. I admired him, not just as a man and a footballer but for his dedication to keeping at peak fitness. We shared many a training stint together and I can tell you it was a privilege to train with such a likeable sportsman.

The thought never occurred to me that I would ever play county cricket. Even then I was conscious of my age and despite inquiries from various county committees I did not believe that anyone would follow up with much enthusiasm when they realised I was nearing my fortieth birthday.

Somerset had made an inquiry about me soon after I went to Blackpool, but I was not prepared to consider breaking my contract. I suppose, too, I wasn't prepared at that time to risk the gamble of being a failure in championship cricket, six days a week.

Nevertheless, Harold Stephenson, the Somerset wicket-keeper, nagged away at his county committee men and eventually I received a firm offer of a three-year contract with the promise of a testimonial after five years. I talked this over with Tom Bradley. He told me that with my average of over 100 I should be all right for many years with Blackpool, but I could not get more than a year's contract.

All the clubs around were only taking on their professionals for one year. They were anxious about committing themselves for three-year contracts at over £1,000 a year, especially at a time when many West Indian stars were arriving and looking for league clubs.

By the time Somerset's offer arrived, I was a family man with two nippers and another coming along. I just had to consider my future. Betty and I mulled it over for two or three weeks and eventually I told Blackpool that if they could not make me a better offer, I would go to Somerset for further talks.

The Blackpool committee wouldn't budge from their conditions and insisted they had nothing fresh to offer. To this day Tom Bradley may still think it was a put-up job by me to get them to give me better terms but I can assure him it wasn't.

When Blackpool re-iterated their decision, I got into my car and drove to Somerset. I fixed up terms there, and went back to Blackpool and told their officials I would be leaving at the end of the season. And when, finally, I said goodbye, I had an average of more than 100.

In four seasons, before joining Somerset in 1957, I hit twenty centuries for the seasiders and established a Northern League record of 1,345 runs in my first season at Stanley Park.

NINE

County gamble at 38

I entered the County Championship lists at the age of thirty-eight in 1957, but my name could have been there ten years earlier. Two fellow Australians, Jackie Walsh and Vic Jackson, who played for Leicestershire, contacted me at Petersham and asked if I would consider a £500 contract to play with them at Leicester.

That was a tempting proposition to step into English first-class cricket, but Colne dangled an even more attractive carrot before me. They were prepared to top the Leicester salary and meet the cost of a return fare from Australia to England.

After Colne had won the battle for my services, the Lancashire coach, the late Harry Makepeace, came over to watch me play in a match in aid of the Old Trafford reconstruction fund. At tea-time Harry asked me: 'How would you like to play for Lancashire?' I replied that it would depend on the conditions and the money they were prepared to offer me. Harry even had a contract in his pocket and said if I were agreeable I could join Lancashire in the following season.

Winston Place, who was a leading Lancashire batsman at the time, was also present at this discussion and we looked over the contract and I couldn't fault it.

Just as I was beginning to think I would sign, Harry remarked that he thought I was too aggressive for first-class cricket. He said Lancashire were interested in me but he'd noticed that I seemed to want to hit every ball for a four or a six. He wondered how these tactics would work out in county cricket.

'Well, it's up to you,' I told him. 'I've made my mark with Colne. I expect you've heard of Everton Weekes. He and I play in the same league and we race neck and neck for the most runs in a season.'

Harry insisted I would have to play more on the back foot if I went to Lancashire. The suggestion hit me below the belt and I turned round, grabbed the contract from his hand and tore it into pieces. Winston Place had heard Harry's remark and he sympathised with me: 'I'd have done the same thing.' I can't say I've ever regretted not going to Lancashire.

The next overture came from Gloucestershire in 1950 via Tom Goddard but they could only offer me £500, with the prospect of the occasional fiver from the sale of a newspaper article. At this time, about half-way through the season, I had earned about £150 in collections with Colne. I was on a £500 salary and I thought I would be a mug to go in six-day county cricket for less money.

Then came a marvellous offer – or so it seemed at the time – from Nottinghamshire. They offered to put me on top money, which was £750 at the time, provide me with a job in the winter, a free house and money from newspaper articles.

This was really a top-class inducement and I could look forward to a benefit after five years. But it was too good to be true. The snags loomed up when we started to talk about my cricket prospects. It seemed that their wicket-keeper was retiring and they wanted a replacement who could go in and knock up 20 or 30 runs when necessary.

I was bloody cheeky as usual and told them: 'From what I can see of your county – you've been at the bottom of the championship for three or four years – it seems to me you need a wicket-keeper who will get a 100 every time he goes in to bat.'

More seriously, I was worried about my position in the Notts batting order and when their chairman said 'six or seven' I thought this wouldn't do my cricket any good. The chairman said: 'Don't worry about it now. Come into the dressing-room and meet the skipper.'

So I went in and who should be sitting there but a great friend of mine, Reg Simpson. Reg asked: 'Well, how did it go?' I replied that I was happy with the money, but the cricket prospects seemed less attractive.

Reg remarked, 'Let us get things straight now. If you come to Nottingham you won't be the top money man, I shall be getting more money than you.' Well, that was fair enough, but it confirmed the doubts in my mind about the job. I couldn't see it working out and I feared my cricket might suffer batting so low in the order. It was a point of honour in those days to talk over your problems with the senior professional to avoid any squabbles when you joined a County. He was kept informed about the negotiations by the Committee. Joe Hardstaff was the Notts senior professional and he agreed with me that I couldn't do myself justice as a batsman if Notts insisted on such an arrangement.

I gave Notts a week to think it over and, in the meantime, back at Blackpool, I received a phone call from Les Ames in Kent. He had heard about the Notts offer and assured me that if I joined them at Canterbury, I would open the batting with Arthur Fagg, who had opened for England and was one of Kent's greatest players.

Two nights later I received another phone call from someone who had been connected with Kent as a committee man for years and years. He told me point-blank that if I came to Kent I would be treated as an outsider and kicked from pillar to post. Now I must say that, as an opponent, I never found the Kent men unfriendly, but I had to consider these words of warning.

This committee man – he wouldn't give his name – stressed that I wouldn't enjoy my cricket in Kent. Clearly he didn't think I was the right type for the 'Garden of England' and so I didn't pursue this enquiry much further. I felt that if he was prepared to take the trouble to phone me, there must have been other people in the County who thought along the same lines as he did.

Warwickshire were yet another of the County clubs which

joined in the chase for my signature, but Harold Stephenson and Somerset finally persuaded me that my future lay with the cider county. They seemed to offer the right sort of security and their offer was so good I couldn't afford to turn them down. Yet for all that, it was still a tremendous gamble for this old campaigner. Somerset, to their credit, never had any doubts about my quality and they gave me my County cap after only four games.

The gentlemen at Lords, who granted me an immediate registration in 1957, could scarcely have imagined that this jolly swagman would score over 18,000 runs and take 732 wickets in ten years with Somerset.

In 1961, when I was forty-two, I scored 3,019 runs, took 62 wickets, and created a personal record I shall never repeat: I gave my wicket away. Normally no right-thinking Aussie would do such a thing, even to satisfy his ailing grandmother's last wish! Moreover, I turned to Richie Benaud, who was captaining the Australian tour team over here, and, in my best Somerset accent, nominated the bowler: 'Take this tripe off, Rich, and put "Davo" on.'

Richie was never a mug; he put Alan Davidson on and I was caught. But on that day at Hastings I'd already passed the 3,000 for the summer, thus emulating the feat of the fabulous Middlesex 'twins', Denis Compton and Bill Edrich, in 1947.

I went back on my life-long principles by conceding my wicket because I was fed up with the impotency of most of the Aussie pace bowlers. Their flabby bowling almost made me want to weep. The Don wouldn't have stood for their mediocrity.

I hit three hundreds and a 95 against those 1961 tourists who managed to retain the Ashes, thanks to Benaud's tactical skill. But the honour that really tickled my sense of humour was to be linked, as an exile from Down Under, with four other Australians – Benaud, Norm O'Neill, Davidson and Bill Lawry – in *Wisden's* list of cricketers of the year.

The summer of 1961 – my testimonial year at forty-two years of age – was a proud milestone in my career and I can honestly say I've never been fitter. Mind you, I needed all my strength for the double century against Warwickshire on the colliery ground at Nuneaton.

We were set 389 to win and our skipper, Harold Stephenson,

called for a special effort. I'm usually a late bird, but on this occasion I had only one glass of beer and I was in bed by 10 p.m.

The wicket was worn on the last day and the ball was spinning, so the knock gave me a great thrill. Everything seemed to go my way, and I used every stroke in the book. It was a marvellous feeling. I reached my first 100 in 29 shots and 103 minutes. The only time I eased up was in the nervous nineties – I was on 95 for fifteen minutes. I finally cracked 6 sixes and 31 fours in an unbeaten 221 scored in 210 minutes.

Colin Atkinson helped me put on 99 and Steve was bubbling over with enthusiasm at lunch. He said to me: 'We've got 'em cold.'

I, too, was confident of forcing a win for Somerset but I ran out of partners. When the last four batsmen were at the wicket with me, I was restricted because Warwickshire had all their men out on the fence. I couldn't get singles. It was either four or nothing. And it was really upsetting to find my strokes blocked. I just had to force the pace in view of the big total we faced. Unfortunately the Warwickshire bowlers were too good for our tailenders and we lost by 47 runs after a great fight.

Records tumbled like skittles in 1961 and Ken Palmer helped me rewrite the county history book when we shared a sixth wicket stand of 265 in 230 minutes against Northants at Northampton. Ken hit his first 100 for Somerset and our partnership beat the previous best stand of 196, established by Maurice Tremlett and Peter Wight at Bath in 1959.

My purple patch came in a trail-blazing eight days when I scored 523 runs for once out. The sequence of scores ran as follows: 183 n.o. and 134 n.o. against Surrey (the first brace of unbeaten centuries in one game by a Somerset player); 13 and 70 n.o. against Middlesex; 123 n.o. against Notts. I was annoyed about that 13. Umpire Paul Gibb gave me run out but I swear I was in by a mile.

The departure of my fellow Australian, Colin McCool from Somerset, put the ball firmly in my court. In 1961 I concentrated as I've never concentrated before. But I was still an attacking player and I didn't neglect my leg-side scythe. There were rumours of threatened strike action by the Association of Short Legs!

I had scarcely time to catch my breath in the breakneck record chase. And I beat the record of seven centuries in one season held by Harold Gimblett, Frank Lee and Peter Wight, with a hundred against Essex at Weston.

My final total was 11 centuries in all matches and I was second in the English batting averages. The people of Somerset said thank you with a £2,700 testimonial.

My pals in the county championship paid me a nice tribute when they voted me 'Cricketer of the Year' in 1962. I received 72 out of the 162 votes cast by capped players – who no doubt gave due consideration to my age when they gave me a big margin above Ted Dexter.

I failed by only 85 runs to achieve the rare double of 2,000 runs and a 100 wickets, but I did vault another hurdle with a career-best bowling performance of eight for 65 against Surrey at the Oval. I think I would have taken all 10 wickets but I spoilt everything by taking a catch in the gulley to dismiss Richard Jefferson. I could hardly have missed it.

Back in 1960, Trevor Bailey, the best bad wicket player in the world, broke out of his defensive shell to deny me the honour of beating former Somerset player, Horace Hazell's world record of 16 consecutive maiden overs.

The game was against Essex at Yeovil. I had been out of the side with a leg injury but I thought I could bowl off two or three paces and still get wickets on this pitch which was one of the worst I have played on at Yeovil.

On the last day the wicket really exploded and poor Essex, facing a big target, didn't seem to have a chance of saving the game. Harold Stephenson nursed me as best he could but I was getting more and more frustrated in the field. Finally I said to him: 'Look, you must let me bowl on this wicket. I only need to take a couple of paces.'

Steve remonstrated: 'I don't want to aggravate your leg trouble, Bill.' I persisted and I think Steve was happy enough to let me have a go at Trevor Bailey who was holding us up with one of his dogged, stonewall innings.

Trevor had settled into a defensive groove and he was clearly intent on staying there until time was called. Steve mentioned that he had kept wicket to Hazell during his record-breaking stint, but I had no thoughts of the record. I just wanted to win my duel with Trevor.

The clock crept round until there were only forty minutes left for play. There were no leg-side fielding restrictions in those days and we had six men round the bat supporting our body-line attack. I remember one player, Roy Virgin, was so close at square-leg that he was sitting right under Trevor's backside.

Then Trevor played forward and the ball lobbed up off the handle of the bat to Roy. Poor Roy never looked like catching it. He put the bloody ball on the carpet and he looked away like a small boy who had been caught raiding the pantry.

Next ball Trevor tried to hit me out of the ground and skied the ball for two runs to break the spell of maiden overs. I couldn't understand the rush of blood by Trevor but I suppose this was a natural reaction after the missed catch.

I think I bowled sixteen overs for two runs – and all the time I marvelled at Trevor's concentration. He was really under pressure and this was one of the best knocks I've ever seen on a bad wicket. He never blinked an eyelid as I pitched ball after ball on his middle stump.

Apart from his one lapse Trevor didn't offer a ghost of a chance and the shutters were well and truly fastened. Ten minutes from time he turned round and said: 'Well, have you had enough?' And we replied: 'We don't look like getting you out.' So we called it a day after a grand battle.

Trevor was a great player on bad wickets and I often wonder how other top-class batsmen would have fared on the dust bowls at Bath, Yeovil and Weston. I remember seeing Tom Graveney and Basil D'Oliviera batting on the Bath wicket. Basil was then in his first season at Worcester. He took several blows on the chest and we dismissed him very cheaply. Tom stayed a bit longer, but he didn't score many in the two innings.

These wickets were real turners and the ball used to spin almost from the first over. But some of the Somerset batsmen used to knock between 1,400 and 1,500 runs each season. In my book this was a magnificent achievement and of greater value than 2,000 runs scored by other players on good wickets. But I would also say, in criticism, that the Somerset slow bowlers should top the averages playing on these wickets.

Somerset are obliged to play at centres other than Taunton to please their membership. They have a big following at Bath where you might not see the best cricket but you can always be sure of a result.

The only time I played at Frome, we had to chase the cows off the outfield before we could play our match against Hampshire. That was in 1961. Roy Marshall tried to hook his first delivery but the ball went straight along the ground. It never rose an inch and Roy didn't have a chance. When we batted Mervyn Burden took eight for 38 to skittle us for a very low score.

Those who advocate taking cricket round the county do not always appreciate the tremendous difficulties involved. A lot of money is needed to set up tents and provide additional accommodation for these fixtures.

Taunton is the Somerset county headquarters because it has the biggest population but I must say they don't support the game there. The local people don't seem to appreciate cricket and many good matches have been very badly supported in recent years.

I would back a move to Bath and I think a case could be made out for giving the status of headquarters to Taunton, Bath and Weston in turn, at three-year intervals. All these centres would then get the opportunity of staging the top fixtures in the county championship.

The apathy at Taunton is shocking – and this applies not only to cricket, but to other sports like rugby and soccer. I doubt whether the majority of the county cricket club members watch more than two or three games a year. They might go along to the games against the tourists and Gloucestershire at Taunton but they probably don't go again all season.

Reverting to my Indian summer with Somerset in 1961, I remember it brought a tempting offer from my old club, Blackpool. They wanted me as a player-coach on a two-year contract. This gave rise to rumours that I had issued an ultimatum to Somerset and had demanded a similar contract.

The truth was less sensational. Certainly I was anxious about my future in the game and I had promised Blackpool I would return to them if ever I left county cricket.

Somerset quickly ended the speculation by offering me a new two-year contract which I gladly accepted. My wife, Betty, gulped with surprise, not for the first time, when she heard the news. 'Well, how long is this going to go on?' she asked.

A glance in the crystal ball would have revealed five more years after that contract ended, three Gillette Cup man-of-the-match awards, and the sadness of defeat by Kent in the final at Lord's.

TEN

Up for the cup at Lord's

The two cider lads from Taunton were not downhearted after the 1967 Gillette Cup final against Kent. I bumped into them outside the Tavern at Lord's. One of them had a big pitchfork stuck through the shoulders of his coat and the other was propping him up in the gutter.

They'd had a royal day in London and they asked me if I would join them in a toast to the county. I'd had a few tumblers of Scotch, gin and champagne after the match, but I was still thirsting for a good drink.

So I accepted a swig or two from their stone tankard which was spilling over with cider. At least that is what I thought it was. I got half of it down before I realised that cider was only part of the mixture. The drink had the potency of a witch's brew and I staggered blindly into a taxi to meet my wife and friends at a swank London club. I couldn't understand the chuckles that greeted my first appearance on the dance floor. Then I saw a trail of straw vainly struggling to keep up with my nifty quick-step.

I must have been pretty far gone back at Lord's, because the playful lads from Taunton had somehow managed to punch a handful of straw down my suit and inside my shirt. I was a bedraggled buffoon lurching around that London nightclub, but it was easy to forgive any loss of dignity in the excitement of this Gillette Cup final which put Somerset firmly on the cricket map.

Tickets for Lord's were as prized as those sought after by soccer enthusiasts on the Wembley trail. The Somerset allocation of 5,250 tickets were sold in five days and the county secretary, Richard Robinson, was bombarded with requests from anxious supporters. He said at the time that he could have sold the Somerset allocation two and three times over.

Old supporters – and even those people who weren't remotely interested in the game – were infected by the cricket fever. They all wanted to join the crowds journeying up for the Cup at Lord's. Somerset even had their own pop group, Adge Cutler and the Wurzals and a hit record, 'Drink up thy Zider,' which had a 50,000 sale after the rout of Lancashire in the semi-final at Old Trafford.

The song and the triumphant words rang around the pubs in Taunton on the eve of the final and Adge and his mates thundered out an encore at Lord's.

'Drink up thy Zider,' went the refrain. 'Vor tonight we'll merry be. We've knocked the milk churns over. An' rolled 'em in the clover. The corn's half-cut and so we be.'

Kent were the better side on the day and they displayed the steadier nerves in this first Cup meeting between the Hops and Cider counties. But we gave them a tremendous fight after almost making a present of the match with some bad bowling before lunch.

I remember taking part in a television preview with Colin Atkinson and Colin Cowdrey at Lord's on the night before the final. I said then that the game would be won and lost on nerves.

The occasion proved too much for our opening bowlers, Kenny and Roy Palmer. They got off to a shocking start and did not regain their control until it was too late. They tried too hard and attempted to break through with extra pace, instead of concentrating on length bowling.

The more they tried the worse they seemed to bowl. Kenny was hit for 18 in two overs and Roy was taken out of the firing

Above: No rest for the wicked – or the wicket! Groundsman Alley at work at Colne. *Below:* My first meeting with Colne in 1948. Shaking hands with skipper Ellis Dickinson. On my right is Mr Frank Wilson, Colne chairman

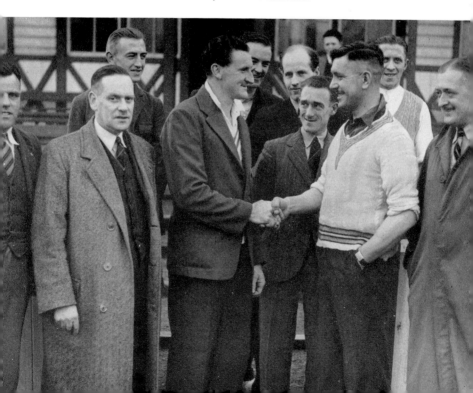

Signing for Blackpool in the Northern League under the watchful eye of the then chairman, the late Mr Frank Plaice

Below, left: Going out to open the innings for Blackpool in the Northern League with my old pal Johnnie Bennett. *Below, right:* Under the Blackpool scoreboard with Tom Incles after establishing a new opening partnership in the Northern League

line after his first five overs had cost him 34 runs. Kent fairly raced away with the game and Mike Denness and Brian Luckhurst battered us to the tune of 78 runs in 70 minutes and 19 overs.

Geoff Clayton took a catch behind the wicket off my bowling to get rid of Denness, but John Shepherd kept up the run-rate and we were in a desperate position at lunch. We didn't seem to have a ghost of a chance. Kent had romped to 129–1 in 38 overs and Cowdrey, Stuart Leary, Alan Dixon and Alan Knott had still to bat.

We pegged them back after lunch and cleaned them up for just under 200. We hit back really hard and Kent lost six wickets for 12 runs in 10 overs. Fred Rumsey made the break when a neat slip catch by Roy Virgin ended Shepherd's gallop.

The big prize of the afternoon was the wicket of Colin Cowdrey, who had just been appointed to captain England in the West Indies. Colin was cheered all the way to the wicket, but he didn't last long. Peter Robinson took a great catch low down at mid-wicket to boost our hopes.

Alan Knott and Alan Ealham scampered a few cheeky runs before they were both run-out, but we had restricted Kent to 64 runs in 26 overs. They were all out for 193 and we thought then that we were home and dry. Our victory target seemed child's play compared with the total that Mike Denness had made probable in the slaughter before lunch.

We had to score at three runs an over – a comfortable run-rate – but our openers, Peter Robinson and Roy Virgin, did not push it along quickly enough, although they gave us a sound start with 58 for the first wicket.

After tea, we really got bogged down and Alan Brown and Alan Dixon bowled four or five consecutive maidens. They bowled really well and Virgin and Kitchen both skied catches in desperate attempts to break loose. Then we lost Peter Robinson who had been in spanking form, and began to get a little downhearted. We could feel the game slipping from us.

Peter, a nephew of Roly Jenkins, the former Worcestershire and England leg-spinner, had been our mainstay and he must have been choked to lose his wicket just two runs short of his 50.

E

The boy had grafted for his runs and this was a lad who had come to Somerset as a leg-spinner. He had been converted into an opening batsman when Tony Clarkson was injured. Peter was selected for the final after scoring a career-best 97 against Middlesex in the previous game.

We tried hard to pull the game round after our slow start, but we had to take risks and the Kent bowling and fielding was too tight to permit any liberties.

A silly run-out ruined any hopes we might have had of winning the game. Terry Barwell and Graham Burgess opened up the gaps in the field when they lashed 27 in four overs. But then Terry attempted an impossible second run and was run out by yards.

Derek Underwood came back to cash in on our efforts to score at the rate of nearly five runs an over and the middle-order batting folded against him. Burgess blazed away until the end – he clouted a six off Underwood – but he rapidly ran out of partners and we lost by 32 runs.

We were sorry we couldn't manage to bring the Cup back to Somerset, but we were only briefly in the hunt after our disastrous start. There wasn't much in it, but Kent just shaded us and they held themselves in control better than we did.

The defeat was a bitter disappointment for our skipper Colin Atkinson, who was playing in his farewell game after seven years with Somerset. But he could at least boast of leading us to our first final and helping to write a success story in the Gillette Cup. We had gone one better each year after our first round K.O. by Glamorgan in the 1963 season.

Butterfly flutters gripped us all at Lord's and I can still recall the bugle-playing fans, the screech of the rattles, the colourful rosettes and the cider lads in their smocks carrying giant sheaves of hay on a day of carnival joy.

Back home in Australia, before I had ever thought of coming to England, I had often dreamed of walking on the sacred turf of Lord's. And when I finally did realise this boyhood dream with Somerset it was almost as if a valley had caved in. I asked myself: 'Is this really happening to me?'

But the real magic of Lord's, with the stands filled to capacity on Gillette Cup final day, was a revelation. I walked out to bat to a tremendous ovation. I didn't realise it at the time but I suppose the crowd – Somerset and Kent fans alike – were acknowledging the fact that the oldest player in first-class cricket was going to the wicket.

I tried to convey to the crowd that I was dead scared after the ovation. And I don't mind telling you I *was* sweating as I waited to take the first ball, watched by 30,000 people. I remember Colin Cowdrey saying to me: 'You've got a lot to live up to there.'

I did get off the mark but Somerset needed a forcing innings from me. I just had to swing the bat, but I failed to get hold of one and Alan Brown caught me at backward short-leg for eight.

They gave me the match award twice on the way to the final. But I must confess to feeling sorry for our wicket-keeper Geoff Clayton who nudged me close for the medal in the third round tie against Northants.

Geoff was really unlucky not to get an award after a great rescue innings. We were wobbling at 116–6 when he came in and cracked up 35 in quick time. Then, when Northants batted, Geoff took four catches, including a magnificent diving catch to dismiss Tony Durose.

We finally totalled 184 and Fred Rumsey struck a great blow for us when he claimed Colin Milburn's wicket with the second ball of the innings. Reynolds and Mushtaq rallied Northants with an attacking partnership but we grabbed some cheap wickets and we won by 36 runs.

Mervyn Kitchen hit 72 in our 91-run victory over Leicestershire in the first round but a place in the final really seemed a possibility when we beat the holders and the much-fancied Warwickshire in the next round.

Colin Atkinson and I shared a 58-run stand to turn the tables on the Warwickshire boys and I then caught the big-hitting John Jameson to check their victory bid. Tom Cartwright and David Brown gave us a scare by putting on 46 runs for the ninth wicket but we finally broke through just in time to win by 25 runs.

Ken Palmer (3–20) was our man of the match when we routed Lancashire by 100 runs in the semi-final at Old Trafford. Yorkshireman Herbert Sutcliffe, the old England opener, was the adjudicator and he probably enjoyed rubbing salt in the wound when he described the Lancashire innings as a 'debacle'.

Lancashire were chasing a target of 211 and Graham Atkinson and Barry Wood gave them a good start with 40 for the first wicket. Then the innings came apart at the seams and wickets tumbled like ninepins. Lancashire lost seven wickets for 21 runs inside an hour. It could have been worse but for Ken Higgs and Ken Shuttleworth who made the score respectable by adding 38 runs for the eighth wicket.

We reached the semi-final in the previous season, 1966, and I was thrilled to receive my first man-of-the-match award in our win over the knock-out cricket specialists, Sussex, at Taunton.

I really prized this medal and it glittered all the more when I recalled that I had collected the scalps of those knock-out terrors Ted Dexter and Jim Parks in a bowling haul of 4–14.

We went on a spree to the local pub after the match and before long I had more problems than Jeremy Thorpe, the Liberal leader, has down in Somerset. I eventually arrived at the rugby club, ate a chop suey and finished drinking gin and tonic out of a pint mug.

The next morning I woke up to find that I had just eleven shillings left out of my £25 share of the Gillette Cup cash prize.

Some time later I went across to Wales and my hosts gave me a marvellous time. They were so generous that I couldn't refrain from asking them what it was all about. 'Don't you remember?' they said. 'You looked after us all night with grog after the match against Sussex.' It was a strange thing. I couldn't remember meeting them!

Much the same story emerged when I went to Hove. Two fellows took me out for a meal and plied me with drink afterwards. When I left them they said, 'Thanks very much for giving us such a great evening at Taunton.'

I really *must* have been round the bend. Still, it was grand of them to remember.

GILLETTE CUP FINAL
KENT v. SOMERSET
(September 2, 1967)

Kent

M. H. Denness c Clayton b Alley	50
B. W. Luckhurst c Atkinson b Alley	54
J. Shepherd c Virgin b Rumsey	30
M. C. Cowdrey c Robinson b K. Palmer	1
A. Knott run out	21
A. L. Dixon b Alley	0
S. E. Leary c Clayton b R. Palmer	1
A. Brown c Barwell b R. Palmer	1
A. Ealham run out	17
D. L. Underwood b R. Palmer	7
J. N. Graham not out	0
Extras	11
TOTAL (59.4 overs)	193

Fall of wickets: 1–78, 2–138, 3–141, 4–145, 5–147, 6–148, 7–150, 8–177, 9–187.

Bowling: Rumsey: 12–1–28–1. K. Palmer: 12–3–37–1. R. Palmer: 10.4–0–53–3. Alley: 12–4–22–3. Atkinson: 7–1–25–0. Burgess: 6–2–17–0.

Somerset

R. Virgin c Graham b Dixon	17
P. J. Robinson c Knott b Shepherd	48
M. Kitchen c and b Dixon	15
T. E. Barwell run out	24
W. E. Alley c Brown b Shepherd	8
G. Burgess c Knott b Brown	27
C. R. M. Atkinson c Luckhurst b Underwood	1
G. Clayton b Underwood	8
K. E. Palmer c Luckhurst b Underwood	0
R. Palmer c Leary b Graham	2
F. Rumsey not out	1
Extras	10
TOTAL (54.5 overs)	161

Fall of wickets: 1–58, 2–84, 3–84, 4–102, 5–129, 6–131, 7–144, 8–145, 9–152.

Bowling: Graham: 12–4–26–1. Brown: 9.5–3–20–1. Underwood: 10–2–41–3. Shepherd: 12–2–27–2. Dixon: 11–2–37–2. Kent won by 32 runs.

Man of the match: M. H. Denness.

Alley's man-of-the-match awards: 1966 – Sussex at Taunton. 38 n.o. and 4–14. 1967 – Warwickshire at Birmingham 45 and 3–24. Northants at Northampton 30 and 2–8 (12 overs).

ELEVEN

Pressures at the top

One of cricket's major talking points is whether the world's greatest cricketer, Gary Sobers, will be able to complete his five-year contract in the County Championship with Nottinghamshire.

I hope I am wrong for the sake of the game, but Gary is now playing cricket six and seven days a week and I keep asking myself 'Can he keep it up?' He looked a tired man at the end of last summer, his first season of Championship cricket, and he does have a suspect shoulder.

The pressure is really on him, playing abroad and in this country, and captaining the West Indies. He has got to keep himself in first-class condition and it won't be easy for a carefree lad like Gary to discipline himself for continuous high-class performances.

Everyone wants to be in his company. It is not just the six hours of cricket but the round of social engagements which are pressed upon him by well-meaning folk. I don't think this fellow can stand up to it. I don't think anybody could. Gary Sobers is the greatest name in cricket since Don Bradman. The Don was a hurricane player and during the time he played no-one got near him as a cricketer, but he didn't play six days a week; nor, indeed, was he an all-rounder like Sobers.

If Gary is to retain his brilliance, both his country and his adopted County *must* find ways of resting him, otherwise I fear he will be burnt out long before his five-year term with Nottinghamshire is over.

Gary is such an exceptional performer that the demands on him are bound to be greater than on lesser mortals. Nevertheless, with the introduction of Player's Sunday League, every player will be expected to contribute more to the game. The public will want their money's worth from this instant cricket and who can blame them, with costs soaring all the time?

Cricket at first-class level is no longer a cheap form of entertainment. Travel, either by public transport or by private car, is an expensive item these days. Then the fan faces higher admission charges and once inside the ground he finds the price of almost everything has gone up. A cup of tea in a paper mug costs him ninepence to a bob; a pint of beer with no bloody head on it (often tasting like vinegar!) costs two bob or more, and another shilling or so goes on a cold pie, which isn't always in the first flush of youth! And, if it doesn't happen to be sunny, there's always the chance of him catching pneumonia!

So the ball is very much pitched in the County clubs' track. They have one hell of a job on their hands trying to make both the one-day game and the Championship matches paying propositions. Already I think the signs are that the Sunday games will probably subsidise the three-day fixtures.

The pressures, as I say, will be primarily on the players. I don't know how the mass of them will stand up to a continuous round of Championship and one-day matches. It may be that some committees will decide to field their best team for the Sunday League and introduce young reserve players for the week-day Championship. The temptation to do so will be understandable if the League draws big crowds.

If that happens it could mean the beginning of the end of the Championship structure as we understand it today. Fans are not supporting the three-day game sufficiently as it is, so they would react even less favourably to a watered-down version.

I hope very much that committees won't be so shortsighted. A three-day or four-day match each week is essential to the welfare of the game in this country. You cannot breed players for five-day Test cricket on a diet of Sunday League fare. I hope, too, that the players buckle down to their new responsibilities.

The most dedicated cricketer I know is Geoff Boycott. He really is committed 100-per-cent to becoming a great player. When he returns to the dressing-room after an innings, he starts dissecting it. He analyses why he was dismissed and how he can avoid a repetition of the stroke, the position of feet and body which contributed to it. This is the attitude which gets you to the top.

I know we can't all be like Boycott, but some fellows think of this game as a comfortable living. They don't bother even to put spikes in their boots from one season to another. They don't think about their play, only their pay.

In the old days cricketers had to serve tough apprenticeships. Today they need only play a few matches before receiving their County caps. Yorkshire are one of the very few counties which do not award them at the first hint of achievement.

If I were a coach I'd tell a young player that he would have to do a lot of work besides his cricket and appreciate what the job meant before he could expect his cap.

He would have to speak to a senior member, both on and off the field, in the right way. I wouldn't tell him to be a good-living lad. That would be up to the boy himself. But I would point out that if he wanted to go haywire, he wouldn't make the grade as a cricketer.

Before anyone accuses me of being a grumpy old blighter let me emphasise that I am prepared to help any lad who has got plenty of determination and is prepared to work hard at building himself into a good player.

It all boils down to the fact that many English coaches are not hard enough. This is a professional game we are trying to play and any professional game should be played hard. They wouldn't tolerate the cricket attitudes at Manchester United or the Arsenal. Right from the bottom the youngsters are blooded for the game and kept in their place.

Often, it's too easy for the young cricketing element today. I never had a coach. No one came to me and said: 'You are not doing this and you are not doing that.' But I've always tried to play the game properly.

I know that I can go out there and bowl six balls on the middle stump, one after the other. I've always done my own cleaning of my boots and pads. I've never used a bat with a piece of plaster on it in my 30 years in cricket.

This is all part and parcel of the game. By maintaining your clothes and gear you are equipping yourself mentally for the battle out there in the middle.

To my mind, the present points system in the county championship is an artificial way of playing cricket. The spinners will continue to remain out in the cold because teams are not going to bowl them against sides chasing bonus points.

You have only to look at last year's averages and you will see that, apart from one or two in the first twenty, they are all pacemen. The seamers are doing all the bowling.

I admit that as a seamer – a negative bowler, if you like – it has been my job to tie down batsmen. This was my living and this was the game for better or worse. I never gave runs away. It was up to the batsmen to make the running against me.

I know this isn't much fun for the spectator – and I'm well aware that he's the chap we're trying to attract back to the game. But I was also responsible to my county employers and I knew that if I finished the season with 50 wickets at 40 apiece they wouldn't employ me.

Again, if I went out there and put my head down and blocked and blocked and got 600 instead of 1,400 runs a year, they would say he's no use to us.

This game of cricket has changed completely. Players today think of the fees of £100 or £150 they can earn in a Test match and the rewards of winter tours. They are playing wholly and solely for themselves because they know there is so much money to be picked up on the side, outside their county salaries.

It is probably a selfish approach to the game, but I don't think you can blame the players. Cricket is a demanding job and it doesn't leave much time to prepare for the future.

I remember David Allen, the Gloucestershire bowler, going on television one night and saying that he couldn't get anyone to employ him during the winter in a big centre like Bristol.

Now for a fellow like David, who had toured the world as a Test cricketer, this seemed a hard thing. On the other hand, you could understand the employer's point of view. He might give a cricketer like David a job and then get the brush-off when the summer came round.

He doesn't like to support a fellow for five months and then be told: 'Cheerio, I've had a winter out of you, now I'm going.' The summer might be an important part of the year in his business.

Down in Somerset, which is mainly an agricultural area, it is very hard to find work in the winter. You can get jobs if you want to slave for peanuts but this is no good if you've a wife and family to support.

Of course, if you're playing for one of the bigger counties, then you might collect around £10,000 from a benefit which could be put into a small business at the end of your career.

But the chap who gets only £3,000 from his benefit is in a much different position. This sort of money won't even buy him a house at today's prices when he retires.

I think the recently formed Players' Association could assist in providing more security for players. As far as benefits are concerned they could urge counties to bridge the gulf between payments. I know there are two classes of player, but the run-of-the-mill county man should be able to say that he will receive around £6,000 as a reward for his loyalty to a club.

The association could also help in establishing reasonable wage scales for capped and uncapped players. I know that many players would welcome the intervention by the association in disputes between club and player. It would save a lot of unnecessary hardship and ill-feeling if the association was strong enough to fight individual cases.

A big drive is going on under the capable chairmanship of Warwickshire's Jack Bannister to build up the cash resources of the association. I can see no reason why first-class cricketers should not have the same protection as their soccer counterparts. A powerful and active association could remove many of the anxieties which bedevil our summer game.

TWELVE

My pal, W. G., was right

Cricket needs its fair swag of discipline but why do county committees put young players in the stocks because they play their natural game?

The story is told of Geoff Boycott hitting a six during his first full season with Yorkshire. He was pleased with the blow until a committee man took him aside and told him firmly that he was an opening bat, his job was to stay there and, if he hit another six before reaching maturity, he might find himself back in the second eleven.

What sort of encouragement is this? The ball is there to be hit, as my old pal W. G. used to say, and youngsters should be reassured time and time again that it is right to play their strokes. This is what the game is all about.

So many players don't get a fair crack of the whip. Averages are a bane, a permanent worry: many committees still judge talent by the figures that are put before them at the end of the season.

This is rank folly. How can 30 on a lousy pitch against top bowling be regarded in cold arithmetic to be less valuable than 70 on a plumb track against cod bowlers. Yet it is. I know for a fact.

It's time for concern in English cricket when the award for

the best young player goes to a South African, Tony Greig, as it did in 1967. And two young West Indians, John Shepherd (Kent) and Keith Boyce (Essex) were strongly in the running.

There is much in Tony Greig's bowling that reminds me of Keith Miller. Like Keith, Tony doesn't know what he's going to bowl next. And, if the bowler doesn't know, what chance has the batsman?

By contrast, the English lad is burdened with don'ts right from the start. He becomes careworn trying to remember what his coach has told him, frightened to fail in case his average slumps and his contract lapses at the end of the summer. Yet he is only copying his wretched elders for most of the time. Young material must be allowed to develop naturally and the players, in turn, must work at the game as did the giants of the past.

Sometimes county clubs make the mistake of persisting with players who are clearly not up to standard. A struggling no-hoper cannot play for his side; he has to play for himself. I maintain a coach ought to be able to advise his committee whether a lad of twenty-one is going to make the grade.

Cricket has never been hard enough for me in England. I often think I ought to have had a dressing down from the captain or the coach after doing something wrong out in the middle. But they never did. Perhaps they thought I was too old in the tooth for that. I doubt if they had ever heard of discipline in Somerset. I remember once, as captain, leaving out Brian Langford after a poor performance against Glamorgan. I had a meeting with the Somerset president and chairman before leaving Taunton for the next game at Bournemouth. I told them of my decision.

They said: 'Oh, come on, Bill. Brian hasn't missed a game for ages. You've got to put him in the team.' I told them that I was captain and I was sticking to my decision. 'Either he is left out or I stay behind,' I insisted.

Brian went into the second team. I know it was a blow to his pride, but I'm sure he benefited from being disciplined. He was man enough to admit his form didn't justify his selection, but most likely another captain would have let him get away with it.

I was a ready-made player when I joined Somerset in 1957, but I was still disgusted at the pre-season training sessions at Taunton. They were a joke. The players knew whatever they did they would be in the first team. There was no-one to push them out, no-one to give them a rollicking when they deserved it.

My idea of net practice was to bowl just as I would in the middle. The attitude was: 'You've got to keep the ball up. You must keep it there, so that they can drive off the front foot.'

Well, I always used to tell them I would never do that when I was bowling in the nets. If a batsman couldn't pick me up off a length and hit me straight over the top of my bloody head, I wasn't going to give it to him. I reckoned it was no good making a feller a brilliant player in the nets. He had to do it out in the middle. I refused to bowl to order in the nets. Even now, when I occasionally practise bowling in the garden, I won't give anything away. I won't even bowl a full toss at the apple tree.

As a bowler, I try to concentrate on every ball, not to bowl as fast as possible, but with the idea of keeping my length and direction. Mentally, over 30-odd overs and about two hours, I get more enjoyment curbing a first-class batsman than I do swinging my bat for 50 runs. Nowadays, I take more care with my bowling than I do with my batting. I know that the younger players are waiting for me to make a mistake and I have found that the better I bowl the better they treat me as a batsman.

Batting is a more natural thing with me. In my book a bad ball is there to be hit. It makes no difference whether it is the first or second ball or whether I have scored none or a 100. Indeed, it got to a stage during my last few years with Somerset when few players fielded close to the wicket to me. They knew that I was not going to play dead bat and let them catch me.

They knew that if the ball was pitched short – I've been known to take a ball from well outside the off-stump and cart it down to fine-leg – that it would be well and truly hammered. Players were aware that anything around my legs would be whacked and a decent captain, who understands the game, was not going to sacrifice his lads and place them in danger of being killed.

Of course, with some players – good batsmen like Tom Graveney – you can sit at their feet and admire their strokes all the time. Tom wouldn't know how to play a ridiculous shot. He plays in the text-book manner and treats every ball on its merits.

I've enjoyed some grand duels with him and I can remember times when I've kept him quiet in the nineties. I've bowled six or seven maiden overs straight off the reel and then dismissed Tom before he got his 100.

We had a healthy respect for Tom's ability down in Somerset and one of our presidents, old Billy Greswell, always used to award £2 to bowler and fieldsman who got Tom out.

I never ranked myself as a stylist in the same school as Tom Graveney or Peter May. Back home in 'Aussie', I used to marvel at the way 'Siddie' Barnes would let a ball go past his off-stump. I would say to him: 'By God, that was close,' and he would reply: 'Look, mate, if you can't judge the ball by the side of your stumps by half-an-inch, you shouldn't be playing cricket.'

But I always thought that the bat was put in my hand to hit the ball and that is what I used to do.

In Australia there was none of the old-time coaching – head over the ball and elbow down the line business. I was never told I was doing this wrong or that wrong. Even when I played for New South Wales I employed the same methods. I was whacking sixes there like hell. When I see some of my old photographs I think to myself: You look bloody terrible.

Over the years I've smoothed off the rough edges, but I've never really had to alter my technique. It might have been different if this routine of mine hadn't come off and I hadn't struck gold straightaway. I might even have had to be content with club cricket. Perish the thought!

But everything has worked out fine. People say I'm an attractive cricketer and you couldn't ask for better praise than that. The fans enjoy watching the artistry of blokes like Graveney and May but they also liked to see the big hitters like George Emmett, Charlie Barnett and myself belting the cover off the ball.

Some people who go to Lord's or the Oval are quite happy to watch good players stroke a 100 in six hours. But nowadays the majority of spectators, who pay their three and four bob to watch first-class cricket, expect more fireworks. If they can see a fellow, a chap like Colin Milburn, go out there and get 20 or 30 – a couple of sixes and two or three fours – they are well satisfied.

Unfortunately the county championship is mostly a grim business and doesn't permit many extravagancies. I remember Northamptonshire's South African, Hylton Ackerman, hitting sixes all over the place in a Rothman's match at Taunton. This was great entertainment for the spectators, but I thought to myself he'll change his style when he starts playing for Northampton. He won't be able to risk throwing his wicket away by trying to hit two or three sixes in the first over.

Ackerman proved my point. I played against him at Northampton and I could see he was trying to hold himself back. I told him: 'You're not playing your normal game – you're too cautious.'

He agreed and said he was getting himself out because of it. But this was the personality of the player. He's the type of lad who will worry while he tries to adapt himself to the county game.

Of course, seamers like myself are not going to serve up sixes on a plate. Take this feller, Majid Jahangir, the Pakistani, who hit 30 runs off an over, batting for the tourists against his adopted county in 1967.

Shortly after Majid had got into the Glamorgan team I was talking to Peter Walker about the new boy. Peter said: 'He's a good player. He's going well.' I replied: 'He's not hitting many sixes.'

'You pitch the ball up to him,' answered Peter, 'and he'll hit sixes all over the place.' He couldn't have put it better – and we both agreed that it was our job as bowlers to put the brake on the six-hitters.

There is a lot of talk nowadays about the condition of wickets. People say counties should provide top-class wickets with a bit of grass on them. Then along comes a bowler who is very fast and he knocks two or three fellows over. The smart Alecs won't have this. They say the feller throws the ball.

I have always said that the first-class cricketer will not play any better cricket on a good wicket. We have one of the best

Above: Just home as Derek Ufton comprehensively wrecks the stumps. Kent *v* Somerset at Gillingham, 1961. *Below:* Relaxing on tour in Tanganyika. Actual owner of the kilt was Mr Gordon Scott on my extreme right. On my left, former England, Yorkshire and Leicestershire player Willie Watson

Above: Alley on tour. Third from the right in back row, in the first Commonwealth side to tour India, Pakistan and Ceylon in 1949/50.
Below: Off on tour again. This time to East Africa under the leadership of Freddie Brown (*centre*), the former England and Northamptonshire captain

batting wickets in the country at Taunton but this does not always produce exciting cricket.

I remember when we played the Pakistanis at Taunton. Little Hanif Mohammed was their skipper and he said to me in the dressing-room: 'Is this wicket still good, Bill?' I told him: 'Yes, the best in England.'

He smiled: 'Good for practice,' and he went out and batted all day for a hundred. This was an example of what I mean. On the better wickets the good batsmen will put their heads down and say: 'Right, I can draw myself up 250 or 300 in this match and up goes my old average.'

You don't get many players trying to hit sixes at Taunton. They are out there all day, five or six hours, digging themselves in for 140 or 150.

Pitches are bound to vary in our climate. You can get a wet season in the North of England when they will seldom see the sun. Now you might turn round and say: 'How do Yorkshire come out on top, then?'

The truth of the matter is that they come out on top because they have got cricket guts and the class of player, including good reserves, who can operate in any conditions.

In their heyday Surrey were criticised by some people who said they were winning their matches on dust bowls at The Oval. Well, of course, they also played away from home. They had an attack for *all* occasions. Alec Bedser could bowl on any wicket. If you laid a blade of grass on any part of the wicket, he would find it and use it.

Surrey had some fine batsmen, but they rarely needed to score big totals. They didn't have to because these chaps – Lock and Laker – could demolish the opposition. If there was just one speck of dust, they exploded on it. And this didn't just happen at the Oval. They were so well equipped that they would exploit any wicket.

Give them a green wicket and Bedser would be the destroyer. Give them a turner and Lock and Laker made it look easy. This is why Surrey won seven championships in seven years.

Cricket doesn't need this constant tinkering with the laws and regulations. You cannot rule the roost by sitting in committee at Lord's and trying to tell players how to play the game.

F

It is high time players were consulted before the introduction of the different points systems. I doubt if there were more than half-a-dozen county players in agreement with last season's arrangement.

Before long we shall need computers to work out the result. I'm certain of one thing. This wasn't the way I played cricket back in 'Aussieland'.

THIRTEEN

Trueman, my blood brother

We're cricket's greatest talkers, Fred and I, and we've had some rare battles on the cricket field.

When we first came face to face at Leeds in 1957, I kept as quiet as a church mouse, I just sized him up. For two overs we exchanged scowl for scowl. Then, loudly enough for Fred to hear, I said to Paddy Corrall, one of the umpires: 'I thought this cock was quick? When's he going to let one go?'

Fred swallowed the bait. I could see his eyeballs bulging out. There was the look of a demented bullfrog about that old kisser of his as he hitched up his bowling sleeve another notch and thrust in his toes. Trouble was brewing!

I took guard. Fred came snorting in and I just froze at the crease. I never attempted to lift my bat from the block-hole and the ball went soaring over my head. I turned casually to Don Brennan, the Yorkshire wicket-keeper, and enquired if Fred had bowled yet.

By this time Fred had followed through in a cloud of steam and defiance. He stood, hands on hips, about three yards away. I looked hard at him and said 'When are you going to bowl the bloody ball?'

Fred swore and, shoving his face close to mine, hissed:

'Right, I'll give you another now and let's see where you can put it.'

I replied: 'If you do, I'll whack you over square leg and out of the ground.'

Even in those early days in the county game, I knew enough of Fred by reputation to anticipate what might be in store for me. I reasoned he wouldn't bowl me another bouncer. It would probably be the old yorker.

As it transpired, however, Fred produced a half volley and I pushed it out into covers for a comfortable single.

As I passed Fred, I said: 'It's about time you put something into your bowling or asked to be taken off. I can't get any practice against this sort of rubbish. It's kids' stuff.'

Our cross-talk act shook Paddy Corrall. 'For God's sake, what's going on?' he enquired. 'It's like a ruddy charity game out here.'

After the first day's play Fred came into the Somerset dressing-room and called out: 'Where's that bugger, Alley? He's not a bad fellow, but he doesn't half swear.'

This young stripling Trueman and I have always a lot in common.

We've always had this vendetta on the field. I pride myself on being a constructive swearer. Fred has a destructive vocabulary.

At Taunton a few years back we were at it again. I drove Fred's first ball and hooked the next to the boundary, a gesture tantamount to tickling a bush snake. Fred reacted with two bumpers and made me wonder whether I was born daft or was merely senile to have provoked him.

The crowd booed and, at the end of the over, I set them off again by striding down the pitch with the bat raised. Fred played along by striding out to meet me half-way.

Suddenly the fans went very quiet as they saw Fred push his face into mine. And out of the corner of his mouth came the promise: 'First pint's on me tonight, Bill.'

Understandably, Fred alarmed some batsmen. Peter Wight of Somerset, for example, never relished the thought of facing him. Once he was nervously pacing up and down, contemplating the ordeal ahead, when he heard that Trueman had been sent home for arriving late. Peter rushed into the dressing-room shouting: 'Trueman's out of the match. Trueman's not playing.' Then he went out and scored a double century.

I remember another time when I brought Fred over to Lancashire to stand in as pro. for me in a league game against Burnley. He had just started playing for Yorkshire, so I asked Norman Yardley if he would release Fred for this game with Colne. Norman said: 'All right, provided you don't bowl him too much.'

The weather, for once, was great and there was a hell of a crowd to see Fred who thought he was on a good thing for a bowling collection. And I thought he was, too, the way he started off.

I'd promised Fred £30 if he finished with six for 30. And I told him I'd take the box round and collect another £50 if he scored 50.

Fred bowled the Burnley opener with a beautiful swinger and he was really hostile at the start. He snapped up three wickets for seven runs but never broke through again. This feller, Peter Kippax, amateur international footballer, another Yorkshire-man, came in and he slogged Fred all over the ground. Altogether the Burnley boys knocked another 90 runs off him.

Old Fred was peeved; young Derek Chadwick had bowled him out when we batted. I think he'd fancied he was going to slaughter the Burnley attack.

Before the innings he had remarked in a casual sort of way: 'When do you think I should bat?' I suggested he padded up around four o'clock. Well, he went in – and over went his old dolls. Derek knocked his middle stump clean out of the ground. You've never seen such a mess in your life.

We went back the same night for a meal and a beer-up at a pub on Ilkley Moor. I'll never forget it. Don Brennan, the Yorkshire wicket-keeper and his wife were over in a corner of the lounge. Don knew that Fred had been playing in this match in Lancashire and he called across in a voice loud enough for the rest of the pub to hear: 'How did you go on today, Fred?'

The reply from Fred was a scarcely audible 'All right.' Don

continued to press the point and eventually called 'Well, how many wickets did you get?'

'Oh, three,' replied Fred, who was getting fed up with all the questions. Don roared back: 'For how many?' And Fred had to tell him: 'Ninety-seven.'

By this time everyone in the pub was laughing. Don was really enjoying himself and he asked again: 'And how many runs did you get?'

'None,' said poor Fred and Don shrieked back: 'Do you mean to say you got a duck?' I've never seen Fred look so humiliated.

I brought him over to Lancashire only on that one occasion. As we parted that night I said, 'Next time, I'll get a cricketer.'

But good on yer Fred – you're one of the best – they don't come any better. They'll miss us!

FOURTEEN

Sent to Coventry

When it comes to talking this old Sydney Larrikin licks the lot. In my time I've talked out Peter May, Tom Graveney and plenty of others. I've been deservedly chided by the Reverend David Sheppard when my tongue ran riot in anger at an umpire's decision.

My chat is deliberate and calculated. In fact, my successes have caused sides to send me to Coventry during play. The first time Yorkshire did it to me I turned to Phil Sharpe and asked: 'What's up, cobber?'

Poor Phil was in a hell of a state. I joked to him: 'You're a bloody little bouncy ball, you know. You want to get some of that gut off you or you won't get into the Yorkshire team.'

'Don't talk to me, Bill,' he pleaded. 'They'll be watching me from the pavilion through the binoculars and, if they see me chatting with you, I'll be for the high jump. They'll give me no peace for a month.' Phil was dead scared because he was under strict instructions not to talk to me.

Northants also took my golden-tongued overtures in absolute silence. But I got my own back when the teams were having a noggin together after the match. When the time came round for me to pay for a round I was speechless!

The trouble with Northants was that they hadn't got over

my jest with Albert Lightfoot whose hooter overshadows even mine for size. I was completing my follow through while Albert crouched over his bat like a hawk, and I couldn't resist rubbing noses with him.

I met my match in Yorkshireman Charlie Lee, who used to play for Derbyshire. Charlie had a dry sense of humour and I never knew when he was taking the rise out of me. This hurt me almost to a point of desperation.

Charlie would clam up when I tried to strike up a conversation in the field. I couldn't get him going and he would turn round, shake his fist and say: 'Look, mate, I'm here to play cricket. Now get on with your game and I'll get on with mine.'

This put the brake on my back-chat and I would say to myself: 'Oh, damn it, I'd better shut up. He's a big lad and there might be a bit of knuckle flying around if I don't keep my mouth to myself.'

In the latter stages of my career the county clubs didn't take any chances. Youngsters coming into the side were warned against swopping jokes with old Alley. 'Don't talk to him,' they said. 'Otherwise you won't be able to concentrate on the game.'

Derek Morgan, the Derbyshire captain, gave me the cold shoulder when I entertained some of his close-in fieldsmen with a few choice stories from my bumper fun book.

Derek's squad of suicide fieldsmen were warned: 'You know, you want to get back there. I won't be responsible for your safety if you get too close.'

I advised them to get themselves suits of armour or take out big insurance policies if they insisted on perching under my bat. Then I really started 'taking the mick' and accused them, tongue in cheek, of never buying me a drink during the whole of my career. 'Look, lads,' I told them. 'This might be my last year in the game – this might be your last chance to show me you're not as mean as I think you are.'

The Derbyshire lads broke up under the strain of trying to keep up with my patter. You could see the smiles at the back of their ears and Ian Buxton turned round to his skipper and said: 'He'll bloody kill us with his jokes.'

Derek tried to soothe Ian by telling him I wouldn't keep it up for long. But I noticed that Derek ignored me for the rest of the innings. I thought he had something on his mind as captain until I realised that he had packed me on the train to Coventry.

It's a hard life but I must stress there's no malice in my music-hall sallies. I don't consider I'm being unsporting. It's even given pleasure to the less sensitive and my gamesmanship has brought me a lot of wickets.

Of course, I draw the line with some people. Charlie Lee was one and Geoff Boycott is another. I would never try to ruffle Geoff when he is batting. He's such a dedicated lad and I think a lot of him as a cricketer. I wouldn't want to spoil our friendship just for the sake of a bit of fun.

I reckon the Reverend David Sheppard will never forget my embarrassment after I disputed an l.b.w. decision which went in his favour. David used to wear the biggest pair of pads I've ever seen. They completely hid his stumps.

In this game I had made a couple of half-hearted appeals for leg-before against him, with no complaint when they were turned down. But, when I rapped him on the pads for the third time, I was sure he was out. I roared my appeal as a formality but, to my astonishment, the umpire shook his head.

At the end of the over I began to let off steam to our wicket-keeper Harold Stephenson with language that would have shocked an Australian barrack-room. Not until Steve signalled frantically for me to shut up did I realise that David was standing close behind me.

It takes a lot to get me hot under the collar but at that moment I wished the ground would open up and swallow me. I started to stammer out an apology, but David cut me short with: 'Get it off your chest, Bill, and you'll feel better.'

I've always had the greatest admiration for Tony Lock. He's a colourful character, mad keen, always spoiling for a fight, and still a great bowler and fielder.

During his first season as captain of Leicestershire he came to my house near Taunton at the end of the first day's play. I fed him royally on the best steaks I could find in town. I treated him like a long-lost brother. We had a rousing evening.

Next morning it was just a memory. I have a habit, while batting, of picking up a dead ball and throwing it back to the bowler. After all, I am a kindly old man trying to help his fellows. 'Lockie', however, turned on me from short-leg and snapped: 'Do that again and I'll have you for "handling".'

There was a mate for you! I reckon he must have picked up that tough talk playing for Western Australia.

In the end, I had my chance to fire back. It was the last ball of the match and Somerset needed two runs to win. Lock spread his field in a wide circle half-way to the boundary. In theory no more than a single could be scored provided the bowler, Terry Spencer, pitched up the ball straight.

Unfortunately for his captain Terry was short and wide of the off-stump. I flashed away and sliced the ball over the 'keeper's head to the boundary. The match was ours, and I hadn't the heart to look in Lockie's direction.

Cricketers may send me to Coventry, but I reckon I've mastered the art of conversation to the point where I can hypnotise opponents into giving up their wickets. It almost goes without saying that you've got to use your wits as well as your skill as a bowler when you are up against batsmen like Peter May.

Take Peter, for example. He's one of three or four Test players I've talked out. Somerset were playing at the Oval and Peter was nearing his 50 when I was brought back for a new spell. I thought I was in for a real hammering by this great player. I realised I would have to try something or he would put me in my place. So I walked up the wicket after a couple of balls and said: 'You know, captain, all the time I've seen you play I can't recall seeing you cut a ball.'

I told Peter that I was going to bowl to one slip – no third man or gully – and leave him a gap. Down I came and pitched the ball just outside his off-stump. The ball might have just come back a bit and as he went to cut it he got an inside edge and down went his middle stump.

Peter walked off with the biggest smile I've ever seen. I said to him: 'Well, captain, you won't get a run if they cotton on to this fault of yours in Australia.'

He was unruffled. 'Look,' he said. 'All I'm waiting for is to sample those lobsters, prawns and oysters. I'll have the time of my life.'

I first played against the boys from the West Indies in 1957 and I have good reason to remember the occasion. We rolled them over for a low score – and they came back at us with bared teeth. At that time, being a youngster of thirty-eight, I opened the innings and faced Wes Hall, then on his first tour, and Roy Gilchrist, a terror of a fast bowler.

The first three balls I received from Gilchrist were the fastest I have ever seen. As the over progressed I was mainly concerned with trying to protect my head. I managed a snick, however, which took me up to the other end to face the giant Hall.

His first three balls were even more frightening. They pitched half-way and reared high at tremendous speed over my head. That was too much for me. I walked down the wicket and said to him: 'You know damn well you won't get me out this way.'

'I know man,' Wes grinned. 'But it sure gives me a kick to see your face.'

Talking about big Wes reminds me of the austerity lunches which the counties used to serve up for our nourishment. I'll never forget the sight of Wes's face when he stepped into the dining-room after bowling his heart out for the West Indies in one game. The paper-thin salad sandwiches wouldn't have satisfied a sparrow let alone appease the hunger of a growing lad like Wes. He wolfed down a plate of sandwiches and then headed for the nearest restaurant in search of more substantial fare.

Lancashire's Ken Shuttleworth is another fast bowler who could follow Fred Trueman as a great character in English cricket. Now that Brian Statham has dropped out of the Lancashire side, Ken will get his chance with the new ball. He is mighty nippy when he lets himself slip and although he hasn't fiery Fred's salty wit – indeed, he doesn't say much on the field – there is something about him which lets you know he's there.

I was batting against him at Taunton when, out of the blue, he let one go at me. Luckily I got a top edge and the ball flew to the boundary.

From the corner of my eye I could see Charlie Elliott, the

square-leg umpire, grinning at my discomfort. I had a hunch that Ken was not quite experienced enough to delay another fast ball, and I was ready for it. It went for four. But Ken will learn – he's got guts and determination.

A lot of fun has gone out of cricket in recent years. The humour has flown with the wind and we're taking ourselves far too seriously. I wonder what would happen now if I repeated the music-hall turn I attempted at Sheffield some years ago. It was a day of showers – a stop-go day which irritated us just as much as the crowd.

After five or six delays I spotted a bright blue raincoat, complete with a hood, hanging in the pavilion. Next time we took the field I put it on over my flannels; on my way out I passed a groundsman who had been putting down piles of sawdust. I grabbed his bucket, plopped it over my skull and began to run in to bowl. The crowd were delighted, but today I would probably be reported to the MCC for misconduct.

I hope I never get too pompous as an umpire but I shall have to watch out for tricks of another kind when I take up my new job this summer.

Right, lads, here's a warning in advance. I shall be on the look-out for those fellows who pick the seam of the ball. I'll be obliged if you don't sneak an unfair advantage over the batsmen. I know all about this particular trick of the trade which propels the ball down the wicket so fast that it might have been unleashed from a cannon.

I used to grow only one nail on my right hand – the thumb nail – when I played cricket and I'd dig up the seam on one side of the ball. Television commentator Brian Johnston scooped my secret after Ken Palmer and I had routed Lancashire in the Gillette Cup-tie at Old Trafford.

He asked me why Brian Statham and Ken Higgs had failed to exploit the wicket as well as we had done. And I fell for it. I told him that I grew only one nail on my hands to any length. 'We used the nail, and our experience of wet wickets better than Brian and Kenny Higgs,' I said.

I remember playing in a game at Bournemouth – I was opening the bowling for Somerset at the time – and I casually asked the umpire at my end, if he was carrying a knife.

He replied: 'Well, I should have one somewhere. I always carry one.'

I was standing there, holding the new ball, and I asked him if he would be good enough to open the blade of his little knife. He still wasn't up to my game and, as soft as a brush, he handed over the knife. I started to cut round the new ball and lightly marked it round the seam.

He at last tumbled to what I was doing. He exploded: 'Bloody hell, what's your game?' I told him: 'I'm picking the seam.' He blew up, waved his finger at me and said he would have to report me to Lord's.

I knew he couldn't do that after being an accomplice in the act and I said: 'You'd look nice reporting me to Lord's after giving me the knife and standing by my side while I picked the seam.'

He quietened down a bit after that and eventually replied: 'Well, all right, we'll say no more about it. But do that again and you'll get me shot.'

They used to take 'the mick' out of Ossie Wheatley, but he could bowl me out with a bloody lemon. He looked as though he had two pieces of lead tied to his boots when he staggered up to the wicket. But this feller used to come away with his five and six wickets and after a fair number of years people began to realise he was not the push-over he seemed.

Ossie wasn't a big-headed chap. He was a great personality on and off the field and I bagged my first pair against him at Weston-super-Mare. He was playing for Warwickshire at the time and he took my wicket on the first day. After the match, we went down to an hotel on the front, downed a few jugs and started to talk about how I was going to get off the mark the next day. After a while I said to him: 'I'll hit you so bloody far I'll kill one or two people in the stands.' He replied: 'No, you won't' – and I cracked back: 'I bloody will.'

We went on drinking for a couple of hours and all this time I was getting more and more stirred up. I could not stop thinking about avoiding that pair. All of a sudden Ossie turned to me and said: 'Have you got off the mark yet?'

I said: 'I'm off the bloody mark, one over square-leg off you. You pitch on and I'll clout it for you.'

The battle was joined again next morning. Mike Smith was standing so close at short leg that I looked at him and said: 'Your glasses aren't getting fogged up, are they?' Mike, who wore glasses, was a magnificent field in this position – perhaps the best in the game.

Ossie started to run up and I remembered our talk on the previous night when I had a few beers across my chest. Down came the ball and instead of me whacking it as I'd planned all night, I just pushed forward. I could see the ball coming up off a length and there was Mike Smith taking the bloody thing off the maker's name on the bat.

I looked down at Ossie. He looked at me and I shook my head and walked off.

Ossie moved on to Glamorgan where they called him 'Dai Peroxide' because of his blond hair and we had another duel at Taunton. I hadn't scored many runs when he came on to bowl at me. Psychologically I think he wanted to get at me and thought: 'He won't last long.'

I glared down the wicket, tugged at my trousers and pledged that I would crack him out of sight wherever he pitched the ball.

He dropped the first, a loosener, outside the off-stump. Again, instead of whacking it, I just dabbed at it and was caught behind. Ossie gave a silly grin to himself and I nearly hit him over the head with my bat as I passed him.

He was certainly my hoodoo bowler. I used to see him in my sleep. But we are the greatest of pals and if I had to be bowled out first ball every time, this is the chap I would like to see do it.

Psychology plays a big part in cricket and in the twelve years I've played for Somerset I can recall different batsmen who wished I'd stayed back in Aussie. They would always know I wanted to have a go at them. I used to tell them: 'I'll be on in a minute. Then I'll give you a couple of runs just to get you off the mark before I do you.'

People like to talk about records in cricket, but I reckon I can boast one that few people know about. I have opened both the bowling and batting and kept wicket for Somerset in the same match against Middlesex and Leicestershire.

The first occasion was when Geoff Lomax and I opened the bowling and also the batting against Middlesex. Harold Stephenson had gone down with a back injury and I put on the gloves to keep to Colin McCool after bowling twenty or so overs.

I repeated the three-in-one act against Leicestershire, at Ashby-de-la-Zouch. I took four or five wickets on a green top and all the time Steve was in terrible agony with his disc trouble.

I told Steve: 'Look, why don't you go off. If you died you would still have to go off, mate.' Steve replied: 'Well, when you come off bowling, I will come off keeping.'

But I was bowling so well that I didn't want to come off. Steve was a great little 'keeper and I reckon this was about the only time he couldn't tell which way I was swinging and cutting the ball.

Eventually he couldn't stand the pain any longer and he had to leave the field. I took over the gloves and grabbed two useful catches.

Ted Dexter kept us waiting to spin the coin before the Gillette Cup-tie against Sussex at Taunton. Colin Atkinson, our skipper, was just about to toss up when Ted said: 'Oh, hang on, I've forgotten something' – and raced back to the pavilion.

A few moments later he dashed back and said: 'Right, you can toss now.' I was puzzled and so was Colin by Ted's return to the dressing room. We asked him: 'What did you go in there for?'

Ted replied: 'I didn't know what to call so I had to consult the boys and ask them: "Heads or tails"!' He wasn't leg-pulling, either – apparently he always checked with the team on his call for the innings.

Do you ever study the mannerisms of players on the field? I always hitch up my trousers when I'm fielding and before every ball. My old Somerset team-mates used to give them a tug as they passed me to take up their positions.

Other players bite a batting glove as they pull it on.

I've noticed that this little fellow Harry Pilling from Lancashire – he's not much bigger than the bat himself and the smallest player in cricket including Harry Latchman of Middlesex – puts the edge of a glove on the edge of his bat as he takes guard. Before each ball is delivered he just pushes the glove and makes a flick on the edge of the rubber.

Ken Grieves always takes one leg when he bats but, by the time you have bowled he has moved right across the off-stump. Colin Cowdrey has his bat completely off the ground when he takes strike.

Some players like to go out to field last or behind the skipper. I am generally out with the skipper. If anyone jumps into my place, I tell them: 'Mind the stripes, lad.'

Before an innings, my old 'Aussie' cobber, Colin McCool, used to get his pipe out and have a smoke. After a while he would put it down and have a snooze. Then he would get up and go straight out to bat.

Other players can't keep out of the lavatory before an innings, and you get some who bite their nails down to their wrists.

I can't sit still and keep quiet when the butterflies are working. I am always larking and joking. McCool used to get on to me about this and I'd crack back: 'Grow up a bit, you are not my size, lad.'

This is the way I relieved the tension in the lull before an innings. Out in the middle I always used to count my first 10 runs, even if they were all single. After that I couldn't tell you how many runs I had scored. But I would count to 10 – and I felt all right. By then, my nerves had all disappeared.

Up up, up and away – the way I like to see 'em!

Above: Goodbye Bobby. Bails fly as I bowl Bobby Simpson, Australia's captain, during the match at Taunton in 1964. At the other end is Peter Burge, soon to be my next victim . . . *Below:* . . . and here goes Peter! No decision needed from umpire Syd Buller on this one

FIFTEEN

Jailed in Athens

The Greeks may have a word for everything, but believe me they probably learned a few more from me on the night they slapped me in jail, in Athens.

There we were, on one of the magnificent cricket tours which my old chum, the late Ron Roberts used to organise. This was something extra special. Ron had laid it on to the nth degree taking international cricket to places where people seldom saw it and making sure that everybody, players and spectators, were going to enjoy it.

We were on our way to Corfu, the first time that international cricketers were to play on that lovely Greek island. Unfortunately, it was a tight schedule and we did not have much time to see the fabulous sights in and around the Greek capital. In fact, we were restricted to an overnight stop and the best we could manage was to visit some of the taverns, to get the atmosphere and try some of the local wine. But for a lad who has been nourished on brown ale, the Greek beverage was a bit rough on the tongue. Come to think of it, not unlike some really rough scrumpy cider.

Perhaps we were overheard being nostalgic for a good glass of beer because we suddenly found ourselves being conducted by an ingratiating guide who was sure he knew where we would find what we wanted.

Ron had warned us that the 'plane was due to leave for Corfu at six o'clock in the morning and that it would be unwise to drift too far. Message received and understood, sir!

Our new Greek friend took us to an open-air café-cum-nightclub. Tables were spread around the stone-paved floor and there was a surround of ornamental walls covered with creepers. Balalaika players were all over the place. It was all very impressive. Some pretty girls drifted over to our table and we bought them a drink.

It was then I should have got the message. As soon as we ordered those drinks several other girls arrived and made drinks disappear like the last swallows of summer. They did not wait to be introduced or even invited. They ordered their own drinks and a wildly-grinning Greek was standing by with the all-so-obvious cash-register-mind ticking over.

I glanced over his shoulder as he was writing and perhaps because all foreign languages are Greek to me I had no doubt that this beaut was rattling all our pockets. I said to the lads: 'The bill is totting up like a bloody speedo' – and we discovered that in about ten minutes young Adonis had us marked up for £25!

He did not like it one little bit when I explained in my most precise Aussie terminology that I was sure he had made a genuine mistake and would be happy to accept the couple of pounds and a few odd shillings which we reckoned was the extent of our orders. Although he clearly did not relish losing the huge profit he thought he had been about to make, he did not press us. Looking back, I was a bit surprised at that and, again, I should have sensed danger.

But if there was a warning signal in the air it was quickly dispelled by a very friendly chap who had spotted our predicament. He had seen us being set-up for plucking and he said how sorry he was that visitors were exploited in this way.

I told him: 'That's all right, feller. The same thing happens in London. If you don't know your way around you soon find yourself walking home because there they will even do you for your bus fare.'

We all laughed about it and wished the Greek goodnight. Almost as an afterthought he called after us and said that if we really wanted a late beer he could recommend us to a place which was truly above board. Indeed, as it was a nice night and he did not feel a bit tired, he would show us the way and even buy us a drink.

Well that's friendliness for you and he really did seem to want to make up for all the nasty things his countryman had nearly done to us. They certainly knew him when he led us in. Again, the much-travelled cynic might have got the message, but we were a handful of friendly chaps who knew only what it meant to play cricket!

However, our smiling, moustachioed guide introduced us but the exchanges between him and the proprietors were almost entirely in Greek. They made a great effort, however, to make us feel among friends. Now when friends get together, particularly new friends, it is surely the custom to split a glass of milk or whatever might be locally recommended.

I think that several of us got the same dawning flash at the same moment. Everybody in the place, it seemed, were tilting their glasses in our directions, with that sort of gesture which says 'Thank you very much.'

When Ron asked for the bill the waiter slapped it down – about the size of a toilet roll and at the bottom . . . £52!

Now Ron was not only the fairest cricket writer I knew, but he was a young man with a great sense of diplomacy and an ability to ease difficult situations. But even before he could begin to state a case why we were not prepared to underwrite this quite disgraceful con-trick, the police appeared, as if they had been standing waiting behind the door.

With a flourish, which permitted no argument, we were driven off to the police station and ordered to pay the bill of £52 and the bill from the first establishment . . . £87 please!

We insisted on being allowed an interpreter and when he emerged, obviously from his bed, he had just as obviously got out on the wrong side because he was not prepared to intercede on our behalf.

Ron realised that we were in a jam. He was angry but worried that the people in Corfu who had worked so hard for the cricket visit might be disappointed. And it was essential to catch that 6 a.m. 'plane. He decided to pay the money – and then the Greeks turned 'bolshie' and said it was too late and that nothing could be done until we appeared before the court at 10 am!

Eventually Ron's diplomacy won, and we got to the airport just in time.

That was a narrow squeak but it was nothing compared with the fright I gave my wife *en-route* for a holiday in Australia. My mother and father-in-law were on this trip and we decided we would like to see the sights of Aden. We hopped into a taxi and had a good time looking round the bazaars. I had agreed a fare with the taxi driver before we started. But when we got back he insisted that we were over our time and put the price up.

I snarled at him and told him I wasn't going to pay it. He jabbered away in his own language. I answered back with some blunt Australian words. We just couldn't get on the right wavelength and before long we were surrounded by six or seven shady customers. They circled us and I looked up just in time to see that knives were being drawn all over the place.

Pop thought I wasn't going to stay long married to his daughter. And the mother-in-law was so scared she couldn't open her mouth. They were really cranky and the wife bawled out: 'Pay him, pay him.' I said: 'I'm not going to bloody pay him.'

By this time the crowd had grown and my new wife and relations thought they were about to witness my assassination. It was only to stop my wife going hysterical that I eventually forked out to get out of the murder squad. It's the closest I've been to getting my gallbladder torn out. I'm certain that if this had happened in the dark they would have had a knife in me and I'd have been dumped off the jetty.

The tale of the suede shoes also rankles with me. I saw these shoes when we docked at Port Said on my first trip to England. They were light-coloured shoes, with crêpe soles, and looked extremely smart.

At Port Said there were the usual horde of cut-throats trying to sell you everything from a needle to an anchor. I took a real fancy to these shoes and they worked out about £4. I bartered this fellow down to about 30 shillings and told him

I'd make up my mind when I returned to the ship. So I went off and did the town. When I got back the trader brought out the shoes again and down came the price to £1. I thought to myself this is a pretty good bargain.

I tried on one of the shoes, size $8\frac{1}{2}$ I think it was, and it was a perfect fit. I continued to barter with this bloke. I kept going up and down the gangplank and he kept chasing me. Eventually I came back and said I would take the shoes for fifteen shillings or not at all.

He gave up the struggle, wrapped up the shoes and I carried my booty aboard. At this time I did a lot of training to keep myself fit and next morning I thought I would have a run round the deck in my new crêpes. I went out on to the deck, and laced up one shoe. I tried to put the other one on, but it wouldn't go near my foot. I looked inside it and the bloody thing was six-and-a-half!

SIXTEEN

County prospects

Yorkshire are the bulldogs of county cricket. They will never admit defeat and they live in an environment which produces champions. I wouldn't say they were better individually than some other counties but they possess this fighting quality which puts them at the top, year after year.

One of the secrets of their success is that they bring in their youngsters at the right time and allow them to mature in an experienced team.

Brian Close didn't have a brilliant season in 1968, but he is the mainstay and watchful pilot of the team. He is the feller who puts the pump under them when he wants an extra effort.

Yorkshire had trouble with their players last year, but this is nothing new. They are always squabbling among themselves. They are always on the boil – and the latest round of arguments only served to forge the drive and resolution which helped them win the championship pennant yet again.

Their batting line-up includes Geoff Boycott, John Hampshire, a very attractive, hard-hitting player, Phil Sharpe and Doug Padgett. On the bowling front there is Tony Nicholson, who is reckoned to be a good medium pacer. Yorkshire also have this chap, Don Wilson, who rarely gets representative honours. But when the ball turned he and Ray Illingworth used to bowl the other team out for a pastime. Don's certain to miss Illingworth this summer, because they complemented one another in attack.

Wilson is also capable of going into bat, when Yorkshire need 40 or 50 runs to win in twenty minutes, and knocking three sixes and a couple of fours in an over. He is always doing something. Yet he is ignored by the selectors.

Derbyshire had a good season under Derek Morgan last year. Derek is a devoted cricketer and a strict captain, and he has brought the best out of his boys. Wicket-keeper Bob Taylor was very unlucky not to get a place in the MCC tour party to Pakistan, but he is still a young boy and has years of cricket left in him. I think he could get his chance this summer.

Essex have a brilliant little player in Keith Fletcher. He has a lot of ability, but he might have been thrown into big cricket too early. Keith has a difficult job batting for a lowly-positioned team like Essex. He was a very nervous boy in the Leeds Test against Australia last season but you must remember that this was a big stepping stone in his career.

Leg-spinner Robin Hobbs is, to my mind, being ruined to a certain extent by playing on green wickets in Essex. If he was playing in Wales or on Somerset's dust wickets at Bath and Weston, he would really hit the headlines. Robin must find it very hard playing in a team of seam bowlers. A leg-spinner has got to bowl day after day, otherwise he can easily lose his accuracy. He is a different class of bowler from the off-spinner, who should always be able to pitch them on a threepenny bit. Robin has to bowl on these green wickets and batsmen can play forward, knowing that the ball is going to come straight on to them. He hasn't much chance of beating the bat.

What a tragedy it is that the leg-spinner isn't given more chance to develop his craft in England, but the present points system in the championship is all against them.

Glamorgan's Alan Jones is another who could be a great player if he was able to bat on better wickets. He has scored a big total of runs against Somerset. Alan hit a hundred in each innings against us at Glastonbury a few years ago, and he beat

Somerset with a century in the second innings at Swansea. He's a brilliant little field.

Jeff Jones is also unfortunate in that he has to bowl on slow wickets in Wales. I remember doing a television show in Wales and I said it was time that the Glamorgan groundsmen tried to help their fast bowlers, particularly those who looked like being picked for England.

I think it is fair to say that Jeff still thinks he is bowling in Wales when he comes across from the other side of the water. I'd like to see him bowl for a full season in England – say on the green wickets at Lord's. He would become a very good bowler and improve his pace a lot.

Gloucestershire, our old 'derby' county, have the best spin attack since Lock and Laker in David Allen and John Mortimore. Allen, too, can be a useful batsman.

John Mortimore is a great hitter of the ball and he is probably the best off-spinner on good wickets in the country.

Arthur Milton is the only player still in the game who played both cricket and soccer for England. He has been playing a lot of years, but he scored 2,000 runs only two seasons ago. He told me there were no ill-effects – the more runs he got the more he wanted!

Hampshire's Derek Shackleton was another fellow like myself – he wouldn't give his grandmother a full toss on her birthday. I like to call him 'Old Man Shack' though I can give him a few years. He has been a great medium pacer over the years.

'Shack' always played his cricket hard and I've never seen him smiling his head off. You would take your life into your hands if you tried to hit him. If you did manage to whack him, 'Shack' would say: 'Good shot' or 'Well hit'. He would then get on with his bowling. 'Shack' was a hard nut, a hard professional.

I used to stir up that fine West Indian player, Roy Marshall, because I made a habit of catching him in the gully. I never made the mistake of standing in the usual gully position because Roy, with his slash drive, would chip the ball over the heads of third slip and gully and it went like a bloody bomb to the boundary.

I studied Roy for a couple of years – if you weren't concentrating properly he could knock your head off – and
decided to stand back an extra two or three yards. I would ask
the skipper to post a couple of extra gullies. As soon as Roy
came out and saw our scheme he would drop his lip – and
that was the finish. If he stayed to get a 100, he wouldn't
mutter a bloody word to you.

Bob Cottam is a tall lad, with plenty of guts but I wonder
how he'll fare now that 'Shack' has retired from the game. Bob
has got to go out and pioneer from one end himself. Then he
may be expected to come back and do some blunt bowling in
the middle of the innings.

When 'Shack' was bowling for Hampshire he would tie up
one end – 25 overs, 30/40 runs and four or five wickets – and
batsmen would say I'm not going to try and attack him. Every
ball is on the middle stump.

They would have a whack at the other feller, who was a bit
erratic. With respect, I think this is how Cottam got so many
wickets. It will be a big test for him this season.

'Butch' White is one of the great characters of the Hampshire
team. He is always talking to you when you are batting . . .
and it is chatter with a double meaning.

He takes one of the longest runs of any fast bowler and at
Bath he walks back nearly to the boundary. The spectators
there are right on the line and if anyone moves a handkerchief,
he turns round and bawls at them in his best sergeant major
voice: 'Stop waving that thing around and sit down.'

This is unmistakably a command, not a request and the
crowd thinks we had better sit down for this chap. He looks a
tough customer. If only they could see him when he starts
running up to the wicket. He is grinning all over his face!

Down in Kent the master, Colin Cowdrey, is an easy going
chap. He has a jovial lot of boys with him, but Kent lack the
fast bowling – a hostile opening attack to take a side apart.

Alan Brown is another of the game's characters. I remember
having a drink with 'Browny' and Kent's vice-captain, Alan
Dixon, in a pub in Taunton. We had a few jugs and 'Browny'
said he was going to the lavatory. Before he went he said to
Dixon: 'Now, don't you drink my beer while I'm gone,' – and

with that he whipped out his false teeth and put them in his pint mug. When he came back Alan said: 'How do you know I didn't drink your beer?'

'Browny' cracked: 'I knew you wouldn't drink it with my false teeth in the mug.' Replied Alan: 'If you have a look, you will find my teeth in the mug as well.' At that the beer was forgotten as they started to argue about the ownership of the two sets of 'munchers'!

Alan Brown fancies himself as a batsman. He once hit me for three fours at Weston and I said I didn't know he could bat like that. 'Browny' replied: 'Well, you only see me bat twice a year. They won't let me bat much because they don't want me to make mugs of the top men.'

Derek Underwood is a very useful bowler when the wicket is doing something. He is so quick that you can't get after him. If you do move down the track, you run the risk of being stumped by Alan Knott, who always stands up to Derek.

England must pick Underwood every time for Tests in this country, but overseas it is a different matter. He will only get wickets abroad if the pitch breaks up. And, of course, that doesn't happen too often.

Kent, unlike Yorkshire, don't seem to be able to overcome the loss of their Test players. Up in Yorkshire, the youngster who takes a Test man's place is really trying to impress the county selectors. Of course, to lose a No. 1 Test star like Colin Cowdrey is a terrible blow to any county. And when you are without a match-winning combination of the calibre of Underwood and Knott it puts a dreadful responsibility on the reserves.

I don't share the optimism of many people that Lancashire are on the verge of a breakthrough in the county championship. They have made the mistake of bringing in six or seven League cricketers and expecting them to put the county on top again. You need a nucleus of experienced players and then you can introduce the boys, one by one, each year.

Leicestershire have taken over the old Somerset tag of the League of Nations. Actually, I think some counties would buy anybody, even a bloody carthorse, and yet they can't win a championship. Yorkshireman Ray Illingworth will be the Leicestershire captain next season and I think he might have made a mistake. It's a difficult job trying to skipper a side and be the main spinner, too.

Jackie Birkenshaw has developed into one of the best little all-round cricketers in the country. He has followed the example of his former skipper, Tony Lock, and plays the game hard. It has paid dividends for Jackie, and I hope he will benefit from having Illingworth in the same side.

This importation of cricketers can be unsettling to other players. On the other hand, it can raise standards. I'm quite sure they were happy to get Gary Sobers at Nottingham. Gary has completed one season and scored 1,500 runs and taken 84 wickets. Some people thought he should have taken 150 wickets and scored 3,000 runs! He has built them up and done a magnificent job, not only for Nottinghamshire, but also for the county championship. The question this summer is how Notts will fare while he is away leading the West Indies on their tour of England.

Not so long ago Middlesex ruled the roost, but the wheel has turned and the decision of Freddie Titmus to chuck the captaincy suggests that all is not well in the dressing- and committee rooms of Lord's. I like their leg-spinner, Harry Latchman. He is a 'beaut' of a bowler and I reckon he could get a job with any first-class county. He could gain representative honours – although he has a Cockney accent he was born in the West Indies – but his colour might be against him when it comes to touring South Africa again.

Opener Mike Harris from Cornwall is a young lad who likes to go his own way and is now seeking another county. His best season was in 1967, when he scored 1,400 runs, but these fellows should hit these runs every season as opening batsman. They have got all the time in the world to settle down and build an innings.

On paper, Northamptonshire have one of the strongest teams in the championship. They've got so many players they don't know whom to pick. Take Brian Reynolds, for example. He has been a great servant of the club, yet he doesn't know if he is going to be selected from one match to another. He is crowded out by the imported players. Northampton take the line that they are paying big money to men like Mushtaq,

Mohammed and Hylton Ackerman and must play them. Northamptonshire have a mature side but they never seem to click as a championship prospect. Roger Prideaux and Colin Milburn are as good as any opening pair in the country, particularly against bowlers who are not doing too much. 'Ollie' Milburn can go in the first over or he can score a brilliant 100. Alas, he is not reliable enough to be regularly considered as one of England's opening bats. Don't get me wrong about 'Ollie'. He is the sort of player people want to watch today. He gets on with the game but how many times are you going to see him score a 100?

Years ago, when Len Hutton was king, you could almost guarantee he would score 50 every time he went to the wicket. This is the difference in the class of batsmen. With Hutton you could take an hour off work and know you were going to see some sparkling cricket.

Surrey will be hard put to replace Ken Barrington now that his heart attack has ended his first-class career. He was their anchor man for so long, scoring his 1,600, 1,700 and 2,000 runs a year and taking the vital wicket with his leg-spinners. They badly need a couple of batsmen to support John Edrich and Micky Stewart, but their main handicap is the crop of injuries which blunts their challenge every season. Another drawback is the fact that they play at the Oval, so near to the head-quarters at Lord's. They are always under pressure and in the spotlight. They have to be on their mettle all the time.

I thought Geoff Arnold had a fine future, but he falls into this injury category. He is always breaking down which is a pity because he is quick and when he's batting he gives it an almighty clout.

Arnold Long is a hard little campaigner and a fine 'keeper but he has been playing for a number of years and Surrey will have to think about finding a replacement in the near future. Skipper Micky Stewart still looks a kid – a fresh-faced boy – he doesn't seem to get any older. He has an unenviable job captaining an unsuccessful side, especially after all the years of glory down at the Oval. In the old days Surrey captained themselves. They were such a great team. I'm not belittling Stuart Surridge but he got out when they started to slide.

Micky has been on a hiding to nothing. I admire the way he has stuck to his job. Others might have told the committee where they could put the captaincy!

Sussex have been an enigma county for years and years. They have always had players with batting ability but their bowling is usually second-string.

Their new skipper, Mike Griffith, is a brilliant field, one of the best in the championship, but he doesn't strike me as an up and coming batsman.

Their South African recruit, Tony Greig, is a very attractive cricketer and, of course, Sussex have a current England fast bowler in John Snow.

'Snowy' has improved a lot since he was first selected for England. He can be quick and he gave Greg Chappell a sample of his speed when Somerset played down at Hove last season.

Roy Virgin, our opening batsman, experienced a torrid spell against Snow. Roy only hooks very occasionally and he didn't like it when 'Snowy' put two or three over his head. He told 'Snowy' that there was a fellow coming in who would hook him out of sight. He was referring to Chappell who like all Australians, is a fine hooker of the short ball. When Chappell came to the wicket 'Snowy' must have remembered Roy's forecast and thought, I'll try this chap out and see how good he can hook. Well, his first ball was head high and Chappell hit the ball too soon, never really got on to it, and it dropped just short of square.

I suppose 'Snowy' thought Chappell didn't play that too well and he gave him another bouncer. This was a bit quicker and it stopped. Greg again hooked too soon and missed it. The ball went right through his bat and glove and on to his face. He fell to the ground, with both hands to his face, and bawled: 'Who said I could bloody hook?'

Someone had passed on Roy's comment to 'Snowy' to Greg before he went in to bat and although he was covered in blood, he had sense enough to show his indignation.

Apart from Snow and Greig I cannot see much evidence of team-building by Sussex. Their tough little left-hander, Ken Suttle – he's around 40 and has played about 300 games on the trot – is still one of their anchor men.

Warwickshire are an interesting side but, like Northampton-shire, they have the problem of whom to leave out to make way for the overseas newcomers. There is a lot of uncertainty and concern here. Dennis Amiss, when he bats at No. 4, gets runs, but he has had to drop down the order to accommodate Rohan Kanhai. Amiss has had to change the pattern of his play and try and force the runs for bonus points. This is why he was out in the cold last season, struggling for runs. He likes to settle down in his own time and build an innings.

Warwickshire have always had a good bowling side and Tom Cartwright is another 'Shack'. He can nail any side down and is a very hard man to get away. Jack Bannister keeps going when he is fit, and England paceman David Brown is a great trier. He has guts but he lacks that little bit of speed which put Trueman and Statham among the greats.

Little Billy Ibadulla is a grand all-rounder. He could find a place with any county today. Yes, Warwickshire should be pushing Yorkshire every year for championship honours but they seem to give up and drop back at the crucial stage in the season.

This year will be a make or break season for Worcestershire. With the exception of Tom Graveney and Basil D'Oliviera, they couldn't be very satisfied with the performance of the team last season. Worcestershire have gone back because they have had the good years of their older players. There are no young players coming into the side and their experienced men are nearing retirement.

So, surveying the county scene I reckon Yorkshire needn't worry over much about challengers. They look the only really professional outfit – in every sense of the word.

SEVENTEEN

You've got to be ruthless

Don Bradman was a hard man, a captain who was not liked by everyone, but he was respected and he had his team in the palm of his hand.

They still tell the story back home of how he directed operations in the field. He would wave you down to the boundary and you bloody well moved, whether you were eyeing a bird in a mini-skirt or not. Bradman was rough, but he got results. I've never seen a first-class captain yet who was thought so much of by his players.

If I were in charge, I would want every man talking behind my back, but not for me to hear. I'd know that as soon as they got out on the field they would benefit from the discipline.

They would have their eyes on me all the time and as professionals they would accept that they were getting paid for playing county or Test cricket and not Sunday School cricket.

Too many of the current crop of English county players aren't serious enough about the game.

We play cricket six and seven days a week in this country. There shouldn't be a country in the world able to beat England in a Test series. Yet we can't pick a consistently successful eleven from the seventeen counties.

Something, surely, must be sadly wrong with the first-class

game in this country for England to produce such patchwork performances over the years?

I repeat, too many players are not sufficiently dedicated. They don't work hard enough at improving their play and some county skippers aren't demanding enough in their standards.

The English county game could do with more men with the single-mindedness of Sir Len Hutton. Len was a hard and calculating captain. He became the complete professional. His batting was as near-flawless as it is possible to get from any human being, and as a skipper, he acquired a vast store of tactical knowledge which he was able to put to effective use when he led England on their triumphant tour of Australia in 1954-55.

No one else has measured up to Len's ruthless efficiency. They reckon Peter May, who trained under Len, was as tough as any Yorkshireman, but how tough was he when the cards were down and he was in charge of a bad team?

I've played against Peter many times and never seen this reputed hard streak. I remember an occasion at Taunton when I scored a 100 off the Surrey attack in each innings. Fast bowler Peter Loader more or less told Peter he wouldn't bowl from a particular end. May let Loader do what he wanted. Now if I'd been captain, he would have bowled there or gone off the field.

Colin Cowdrey is another player who lacks 'steel' in his make-up as a captain. As an England leader, you have got to be in the position to give the team a good rollicking. Colin is a master batsman who has done England proud, but, to my mind, he just hasn't the qualities to be ruthless. At Test level, you can't be a decent chap all the time – at least not if you want to thrash the living daylights out of your opponents.

Some Test players need driving. They don't respond to the 'Good Shot' and 'Well done, old chap' routine.

Bill O'Reilly, who captained New South Wales, was a hard nut when commanding a side. He liked his jar of grog but as soon as he got out on the field he did his job as bowler and captain.

I remember one time when we were down at the Cricketers' Club in Sydney before a match against Bill's club, St George's.

Left: A helping hand from Richie Benaud. Richie signs a bat to be auctioned for my testimonial during the 1961 Australian tour

Below: That was a six that was. Batting against Sussex, with Mike Griffith behind the wicket

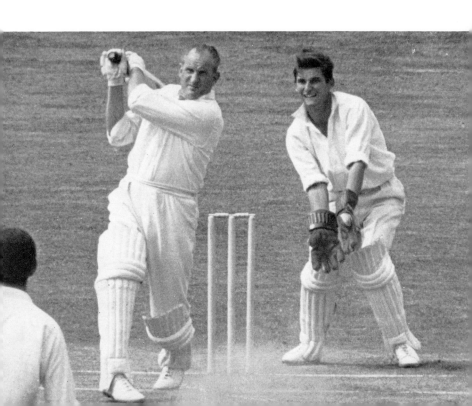

Left: Another trophy for the shelf: for the 'outstanding cricketer of the year in 1961.' This time £500 went with the trophy

Below: Holding the trophy awarded for scoring 3,000 runs in 1961. Clutching the bowling award is Tony Pearson (Cambridge University) for taking all 10 Leicestershire wickets

We were having all the fun in the world over a drink or two. But afterwards when we drove through the gates into Petersham cricket ground, Bill turned round and said, 'Right, this is where the fun stops. From now on we are enemies.'

Old 'Tiger' O'Reilly influenced me in a big way. I always kept it in my mind that although you can lark about, you must keep your sense of balance when the pressure is put on you at cricket. I thought of this again when I believed I was going to get the captaincy of Somerset in 1965.

The county approached me when Harold Stephenson had to call quits because of a back injury. I was prepared to accept the captaincy on the understanding that I would be given a free hand with regard to team selection and the fitness of the players. The club president, Billy Greswell, chairman 'Bunty' Longrigg and secretary Richard Robinson were all in agreement with my conditions but they asked me not to say anything about the captaincy until it had been approved by the executive committee.

I took over as acting captain in the third match of 1964, and skippered the side right through that season. I was the Somerset representative at a captain's meeting at Lord's and told them, unofficially, that I would be skipper in the following season.

The whole thing was very hush-hush. We kept it to ourselves, the wife and I. We didn't even tell our relations in case it leaked out.

Then the executive committee met. They knew me as an outspoken chap and I didn't always see eye to eye with some of the members of the committee. Next morning I received a 'phone call and a very apologetic letter from Bill Greswell, who told me that I had been out-voted and Colin Atkinson was to be the new captain.

Mr Greswell was desperately sorry about the change of plan and I am convinced that the decision was taken against his wishes. I immediately rang Colin Atkinson and congratulated him.

Colin, who understood my disappointment, said he hoped I would continue in county cricket and play under him. I had never had anything in black and white about the captaincy and there was really nothing I could do about it. As a professional cricketer, I had to smother my pride and take a back seat again but not before I was inundated with calls from the London papers asking for my reactions. I made a statement to the effect that Somerset had played a dirty trick on me. The newspaper boys also got in touch with the secretary and he told them that I had no right to surmise anything about the captaincy.

I suppose the truth of the matter was that Somerset thought I would insist on a complete shake-up of the club. They were frightened I would upset the applecart – and they were right. I couldn't see any future for the county unless there was a big alteration in the running of the club. Certainly, I would have insisted on improving coaching methods. In my view the system was too lackadaisical. My boy, Ken, was a useful cricketer and could have joined Somerset, but I advised him against the move.

At the time he was appointed captain I didn't think Colin Atkinson was a good enough player to hold his place in the Somerset side, but he proved me wrong by scoring over 1,000 runs as a No. 6 batsman. He was also a good leg-break bowler. It was a pity he had to have an operation on his fingers and this restricted him as an all-rounder.

After he was made skipper Colin frequently consulted me first before making any major decision. I had turned down the job as senior professional so if we made a mistake it was Colin who got the kick in the pants from the committee. He was severely handicapped by a back injury and his hand trouble, and it was a terrible thing watching him try to keep his form at the finish.

Colin kept the captaincy for three seasons and then the job was given to another amateur, Roy Kerslake. I never understood the logic of that appointment, but I wasn't surprised when Brian Langford was asked to do the job this summer. At least he's had years of county cricket experience. Roy had played virtually no county cricket and it was absurd and unfair to the man to expect him to make a success of it.

Personally, I can't see any strength or bloody guts in making a man skipper just because he is an amateur. Maybe it is because committees think they can dictate to these fellows.

Somerset have always had the image of being a happy-go-lucky county – a jovial team that plays the village green type cricket – and, wrongly in my view, they have perpetuated the rule of the easy-going captain.

They have rarely had a skipper capable of making the county a force in the championship. The best in my time with the county were two professional players – Maurice Tremlett and Harold Stephenson.

Maurice was the best captain I played under. He had played championship cricket for many years and he knew the rights and wrongs of the game and the weaknesses of our rivals. I never agreed with people who said that Maurice didn't care a hoot about the result of a game and that he was more concerned with working out race results and picking the winners.

He knew my strength as a bowler and the right time to take me off, irrespective of my views. He would say: 'Right, put your sweater on' – and that was the end of the matter.

He might bring me back after three or four overs and in my own mind I would say: 'Well, he has done the right thing.' I often used to think that if Maurice had possessed top-class bowlers, he could have been one of the best leaders in the country. He was completely unflappable and if we were having a rough day, he would say: 'Well, lads, we can't push this brick wall over. But keep on trying.'

Harold Stephenson was a different personality altogether. He was really too nice a lad, too good a mixer and too much of a worrier to do the job. The blokes respected Steve but he used to get up in arms so quick. Steve wanted a wicket with every ball and if you were off target, he would tell you: 'You can see the three stumps are there. So why don't you bowl at them?'

Steve hated to give a run away and he would kill himself as a batsman, dashing between the wickets instead of pacing himself. Poor Steve hurt himself more than the team. He so desperately wanted good results and, unlike Maurice, he couldn't understand why the brick wall didn't topple over.

EIGHTEEN

Room at the top

A lot of people say that the Australian selectors sent too many youngsters on the tour of England last summer (1968).

That's true – they had to. The established hands who have been on tours and who are still full of cricket, are being enticed away from the game by big money offers. The cash is far in excess of anything they would receive for touring England. That's why so many are retiring from Test cricket at an early age. They say: 'To hell with records. We're losing money by remaining in the game.'

One typical example is former skipper, Bobby Simpson. Bobby is still a great player, capable of scoring many more runs on the international roundabout. But you can't blame him for accepting a well-paid job. He has got to look to his future.

I am certain the Australian players will use Test cricket as a short-term step to a good business future. They will play big cricket over a shorter period.

The 'Aussies' paraded a good young team in 1968, but many of their players failed to adapt themselves to English conditions. The one big exception was Ian Chappell. He had some experience of league cricket in England, and he got his head down and played the game as it needs to be played over here.

I reckon Australia ought to be grateful to young Chappell

and his skipper, Bill Lawry. They scored an awful lot of runs and steered their side to victory in a number of games.

In England, the selectors are engaged in their own desperate search for young batsmen. The chance is there for a top-class youngster to stake his claim for Test recognition. The prospects of promotion couldn't be brighter, particularly in view of the near-certain retirement from Test cricket of England sheet anchor Ken Barrington after his heart attack in Australia.

Many bowlers will sympathise with Ken after his illness, but they will also breathe a sigh of relief at the departure of this granite-like defender of England's causes. Barrington was never an easy player to prise out and I know, as a bowler, that there is nothing worse than to face a batsman snarling defiance at you for two days.

All of us in the pace brigade would prefer to bowl at the fellow who puts the accent on attack. We will suffer being lashed for 50 or 60 by Dexter or Milburn rather than bowl ourselves into the ground against the Barringtons of this world.

Tom Graveney, the great stylist of post-war cricket, must be close to going back after his Indian summer with England. He and Boycott and more recently, John Edrich have carried the England batting on their shoulders and young men like Dennis Amiss and Keith Fletcher must now make their challenge.

Fletcher is the ideal player to come in and force the pace. The trouble seems to be at the moment that he is too aggressive – he doesn't allow himself time to settle down. Amiss, on the other hand, is in the Barrington mould. He is the compiler of runs. He gets into one gear, and won't accelerate.

There could be room for both of these players in the England team. But you still need the stylist, the aggressive player to push the score along. This is what the game is all about. It is no use batting for three days and thinking you can bowl out the other side twice in the next two days. This lack of enterprise, putting the onus on the opposition, is one of the evils of English cricket today.

Looking ahead to Test series in the next decade, I can see Yorkshire's Geoff Boycott as a successor to Colin Cowdrey as the England captain.

Roger Prideaux of Northampton has a lot of supporters but I would like to see the position given to Boycott. Geoff is a very sensible and stable young player and he has a shrewd head. He has been brought up in the right school and taught how to play hard cricket with Yorkshire.

England, like the West Indies and Australia, must now think in terms of rebuilding their team. We cannot rely on the veterans for very much longer, and I would like to see the selectors putting their faith in youth as an investment for the future.

Boycott, Edrich, Prideaux, Milburn, Graveney, Amiss, Fletcher, David Green and Eric Russell would be my main batting choices for the 1970 series against South Africa in England. But I would spring a surprise here by bringing in my old team-mate, Mervyn Kitchen of Somerset. Mervyn has only to keep up his improvement in recent seasons to make a bid for an England place.

Alan Knott of Kent has established himself as No. 1 wicket-keeper, but he will face a determined challenge from young Bob Taylor of Derbyshire. Jeff Jones, John Snow and David Brown will still form the basis of our pace attack and the spinners are likely to come from Derek Underwood, Robin Hobbs, Harry Latchman and Pat Pocock.

I have said that Tom Graveney must be nearing retirement, but you cannot write him off for the 1970 series. After all, who would have thought that he would make such a tremendous come-back to Test cricket in the last few series?

At this moment of time I can see no reason to discard Tom – he's still only a youngster compared with Alley, the ageing wonder. Tom has such a superb technique – and so far shows no sign of flagging. He could go on for another two or three seasons.

The selectors will probably rely on the older school of players if they maintain their fitness and form. This policy will be wrong unless they also blood young players in preparation for the tour of Australia in 1970–71.

I appreciate that the absence of suitable candidates must be a worry to the selectors. And right here and now I would find it hard to pick a party of sixteen or seventeen players for the tour. Selecting the top five batsmen for Australia would be an even more difficult problem. David Green of Gloucestershire had a great season last year, but his fitness is suspect for a long tour; John Hampshire of Yorkshire can be a magnificent attacking batsman, but he lacks consistency; Colin Milburn is plagued by weight trouble; and Dennis Amiss still has to prove himself as a Test player.

On the bowling front, we have the right calibre of pacemen and Alan Ward of Derbyshire could force himself into the reckoning. He didn't play against Somerset last season, but other players tell me he is nippy, though erratic.

We shall be in a better position to talk about his prospects after he has played a full season this summer (1969). He may make the grade, but he won't be any good for Australia if he breaks down halfway through the season. Freddie Trueman said the other day that you've got to have strong legs and a strong back as a fast bowler: without them you might as well forget your ambitions.

David Brown may not rank among the greats as a Test bowler but he has a heart as big as a lion and he's a strong lad. There isn't a bigger trier in the game than David.

The cancellation of England's tour of South Africa last winter was a tragedy for the game, but I can see no reason why the Springboks should not be allowed to visit England next year. They will come to play cricket and not to talk politics. As far as I'm concerned, the more they keep politics out of sport, the better it will be for all games.

Racial problems – whether you vote Tory or Labour – and the internal constitutions of countries have nothing to do with cricket. If you introduce political considerations, there is bound to be ill-feeling and people will erupt because these are emotional problems. I appreciate it is easy to get involved in political controversy. We experienced this during a Commonwealth tour of East and South Africa a few years ago. They asked us if we were interested in the political side directly we got off the plane. We didn't mince our words. We told them we had come to play bloody cricket. Wes Hall and Charlie Griffith were in the party and both played in our games in East Africa.

Basil D'Oliveira was unfortunate to get involved in the uproar in 1968. I think a lot of first-class cricketers thought he ought to have been picked in the first place, but I still feel that the MCC should have toured without him if necessary. Indeed, Basil might have preferred to be omitted from the team. He is a good sportsman and I feel he may well have felt he was stepping on the corns of the rest of the team.

I think the reason why the MCC didn't pursue the question of D'Oliveira's selection originally was because they didn't think his form merited a place in the tour party. He had a bad season in the county championship, and my own view is that one century in a Test match doesn't make you a champion. On his overall form 'Dolly' wasn't entitled to go on the tour. In my opinion he was selected as the result of high pressure tactics by newspapers – they got him in – and because of the row which the publicity aroused the MCC were forced to make a stand on the racial issue.

Harry Latchman, the Middlesex leg-spinner, another coloured lad, is making a strong claim for an England place – and he could be involved in another political storm. However, I think the MCC will have learned their lesson. Selection issues of this nature should be thrashed out well in advance next time.

But I still hark back to my first point that the game of cricket should be greater than the man. And I believe the MCC should tour South Africa, even if the South African authorities refuse to accept a coloured player.

If we go on involving cricket in politics, we could find ourselves on a very sticky wicket. India, Pakistan, the West Indies and even Australia, who pursue an all-white population policy, could all raise objections to playing us because of political dissension of one kind or another. MCC's role, surely, is to keep cricket alive internationally. We shan't do that if we put politics first.

The West Indies are going to find it very hard to replace those great fast bowlers, Charlie Griffith and Wes Hall. I can't see any replacements, nor can you expect Gary Sobers to step into the breach as opening bowler and then go on and bowl his spinners after probably making a 'ton' with the bat.

The only real discovery in the Caribbean has been the

emergence of Clive Lloyd, who is now qualifying for Lancashire. He will be a big draw with the West Indies this summer.

Seymour Nurse, who has long been considered a great batsman, should now begin to make an impact on the Test scene.
Nurse has had to take a back seat to Kanhai and Sobers for
many years and he is in a similar position to that of Clyde
Walcott during the era of the three W's.

Walcott was in the background while Worrell and Weekes
stole the headlines, but when they got out he took over as star.
Similarly, Nurse has been waiting in the wings as understudy
to Sobers and Kanhai.

Talking about great cricketers, I have had the good fortune
to play with and against some of the all-time best in Australia.
My finest 'Aussie' team would include Bill Ponsford, Bill Wood-
full, Bradman and Stan McCabe. And my bowlers would com-
prise those ace spearheads, Ray Lindwall and Keith Miller, with
Bill O'Reilly and Clarrie Grimmett in support. Bertie Oldfield
would be my first choice behind the stumps.

Grimmett would be my preference over Fleetwood Smith,
the chap whom they said looked like Hitler and made his own
conquests in his day. This feller, Fleetwood Smith, could spin
the ball a mile and baffle the best batsmen. But there were
times when he couldn't pitch a length, and then they murdered
him.

Clarrie Grimmett once told me that he spent four years per-
fecting one particular ball before he bowled it in the middle. He
would go behind the pavilion, where no-one could see him, and
work away at developing this new type of delivery.

Another great Australian bowler, Arthur Mailey, always
maintained that he could bowl full tosses with the new ball and
still get wickets. He used to say there was nothing worse than a
full toss coming in at you at an angle so that you had to play
it. He argued that if the ball was delivered in the right way,
batsmen couldn't avoid hitting it in the air.

Len Hutton and Cyril Washbrook go straight into my best
England side. I would place Washbrook above Boycott because
he was one of the best cover fieldsmen in the world.

Bill Edrich and Denis Compton, Peter May or Colin Cowdrey,
would be my other batsmen, and Trevor Bailey would come in

as the all-rounder. You couldn't leave Trevor out of any team picked at the time he was playing.

Springheeled Jack, Godfrey Evans, a happy personality and acrobatic catcher of a ball, is a 'must' behind the wicket. The spin attack would be in the hands of Tony Lock and Jim Laker, and Alec Bedser, Brian Statham and Fred Trueman would get my vote in the pace charts.

Tom Graveney might come in as an extra batsman and a case could be made out for Ted Dexter, a similar type of player to Keith Miller. Bailey might be included in Edrich's place.

I've had to leave out Ken Barrington. I know he has got a vast amount of runs for England, but Colin Cowdrey would come first among the players still in the game today.

You must remember that I am picking a team from the players I have known during twelve years in county cricket. It's a hard choice to make, but I must stand by the players who put England right at the top of the tree.

By the way, I don't suppose I was the only one to be fed up because Fred Trueman did not get an award in the 1969 New Year's Honours List. Whoever said 'no' must have been joking. If I were a betting man I would have a bob or two on Fred's name being in the next Honours List.

NINETEEN

My greatest match

They roared me back to the pavilion after I had defied my Aussie cobbers and saved Somerset from having to follow on at Taunton in June 1961. Old man Alley was a weary feller after a grim duel with the tourists but it was the biggest thrill of my career – the moment I had been waiting for since stepping up into the county game.

I had entered that particular match determined that I would master the kids from Down Under and leave them with a memory they would never forget. The Aussies were just as keen to see the back of me and I was still waiting to get off the mark when wicket-keeper Barry Jarman shrieked to the heavens for a catch behind the wicket.

The crowd was stunned but I knew I hadn't played the ball – it had glanced off my belly button as it went through to Jarman – and I stood my ground. The umpire never hesitated. He gave me 'not out' and I went on to score a ton.

This was my fifth hundred of the season and my final tally of 134 was only two runs short of the highest score ever made by a Somerset player against the Australians. M. D. Lyon, the Cambridge University and Somerset player, hit 136 against the 1926 tourists.

That hundred hoisted me to the top of the national averages

for the first time in my county career and I hit two sixes, one five and 22 fours in an innings which lasted three and a half hours.

The loudspeaker crackled into action when I got into the nervous nineties. The speaker boomed out: 'A collection will now be taken in aid of Bill's testimonial fund.' This was a nice piece of psychology. The chink of coins in the buckets relieved the tension and I duly passed my 100. They told me later that the collection had realised £221 which, added to the £136 taken on the previous day, provided a grand bonus.

Mervyn Kitchen hit 31 while helping me put on 93 for the fifth wicket and when he got out I let fly and cracked 19 off five balls from left-hander Ian Quick. We still needed seven runs to save the follow-on when our last man, Ken Biddulph joined me at the wicket. I managed to farm the bowling and eke out the vital runs before being caught off a skier.

Barry Jarman claimed four victims behind the wicket and Lindsay Kline, who bowled really well, took five for 89 in the Somerset first innings.

We had felt the full weight of the Australian batting machine in the tourists' first innings. Colin McDonald and Brian Booth knocked up centuries and Bill Lawry hit 70 as they totalled 440 for only three wickets down.

The Australians were all out for revenge in our second innings, but I was just as stubborn and I failed by only five runs to become the second player to score two centuries in an English match against the Australians. My old mate, Colin McCool, was similarly unlucky. He just failed to score two hundreds for Somerset against the Aussies in 1956.

The Taunton ground lived up to its reputation as a batting paradise in the 1961 game against the Australians. Our grounds-man had excelled himself and the crowd, basking in glorious sunshine, were treated to a feast of runs. Nearly 1,200 runs were scored in the three days and my contribution left me only 61 runs short of a 1,000 runs in June.

Despite the batting supremacy, the Australians came mighty close to bowling us out twice. Only a last-ditch effort by our last pair, Brian Langford and Ken Biddulph, saved us from defeat in the second innings.

Even in such a nail-biting situation there were moments of light relief from those closing overs. The 'Aussie' fast bowler, Ron Gaunt, had trouble with his run-up, was twice called for dragging and twice failed to deliver the ball. Amid all the confusion umpire Paul Gibb lost count of the number of legal deliveries sent down by Gaunt!

I scored another 100 against the 'Aussies' in the Hastings festival, but the pressure was off by then. I had passed the milestone of 3,000 runs for the season and I was living in a dream world of telegrams and congratulations from all parts of the globe.

The Australian match at Taunton was a great memory, but the game against Surrey, in which I scored two unbeaten hundreds, ran it close. I scored 317 in the two innings and Peter May threw out a tantalising challenge when he asked us to score 271 for victory in three hours in the second innings.

He paid our batsmen quite a compliment, but Peter was shrewd enough to realise that the wicket was stuffed with runs. Brian Roe hit 42 and Geoff Lomax played a merry little innings. However, we were dropping behind the clock when Harold Stephenson came out to join me at the wicket.

Steve and I had a quick chat to assess the situation. Time was running out and the Surrey fieldsmen were dotted around the boundaries to stop the fours. I broke the tension with a sixer over the ropes and soon afterwards I swept Gibson to the boundary to give us victory by four wickets and three minutes to spare.

This was a real thriller of a game and I struck two sixes and 17 fours in the hectic run chase. My hundred came in ninety minutes to beat Ron Tindall's fastest hundred of the season, scored earlier in the day.

I hit my eighth century of the season – one more than any other Somerset player – to bring my aggregate to 2,317 runs and beat Peter Wight's tally of 2,316 made in the previous season.

Another landmark in a season which exceeded my wildest dreams was a furious 'ton' against the Yorkshire 'bulldogs'. I always delighted in giving the Yorkshire lads a caning and I hammered them for an unbeaten 155 after Fred Trueman had taken two for 13 in his opening spell at Taunton.

Left-hander Keith Gillhouley was my particular target. I hit him for three sixes, including two in succession, and one of them landed in the churchyard behind the long-on boundary.

Geoff Lomax and I shared a stand of 184 for the fourth wicket against Yorkshire and I boosted my aggregate for the season to 1,707 runs.

This spurt of run-getting came after a poor season in 1960 when I could manage only 741 in 41 innings.

I think one of the reasons for the transformation was the departure of Colin McCool from Somerset. I realised then that Somerset needed an extra effort from me, so I curbed my unorthodox swinging and started getting my head down as a sheet anchor batsman.

Nothing gave me greater pleasure in my record-breaking season than to find my name bracketed with those all-time greats, Jack Hobbs and Frank Woolley, after establishing a Somerset record of 11 centuries in one season.

Hobbs and Woolley, as I mentioned briefly earlier in the book, are the only other players to have scored more centuries after the age of 40. Hobbs was 42 when he hit 16 hundreds in 1925 to pass W. G. Grace's record of 126 centuries in first-class cricket. The great Surrey and England batsmen also hit 12 hundreds when he was 45 in 1928 and 10 hundreds three seasons later. Frank Woolley totalled 11 centuries in his 43rd year and he was still the pride of Kent in 1934 when he hit 10 centuries at the age of 47.

Please don't mistake my meaning when I make these comparisons. I don't put myself in the category of these great cricketers. But it is a comforting thought that my name is alongside their's in the record book.

The 1961 game against my Aussie cobbers certainly was my greatest match. Few people will argue about that. When it comes to settling Somerset's greatest-ever season since they started championship cricket in 1891 I wouldn't mind betting there would be a few punch-ups before the issue was settled.

I might have been lucky enough to have played a part in the best-ever season. By my reckoning it must have been in the summer of 1958. It was certainly the best year statistically. We finished third behind the all-conquering Surrey and Hampshire – the highest position in the history of the county.

I know that long before my time Somerset finished third in 1892 in only their second year of championship cricket. But in those early days there were only another 11 teams in the race.

In my second year of championship cricket we had sixteen other sides trying to cut us down to size. Most of them failed because we managed to win twelve of our twenty-eight matches. I reckon we could have finished above the lot of them if our batting had proved up to the mark in times of a crisis.

Those were the days when the rest of the counties would take the micky out of Somerset. We were known as the 'League of Nations' side. Not one of the established county players was born inside the Somerset boundary.

It was that happy era when Maurice Tremlett managed to mould a group of outsiders together to have faith in one another, belief in themselves and pride in their adopted county – very much the type of job the late Sir Frank Worrell did for the West Indies in the early sixties when he persuaded the West Indies players to forget their inter-island rivalries and jealousies and play as one complete unit. Not that we were a bunch of jealous individuals, it was just that we were so very different. The only common denominator was cricket.

Our batting was full of ups and downs, like a switchback at a funfair, and just as heart-stopping at times. We were just as liable to make 300 plus in an innings as be bowled out for around the 60 mark. In fact only the three imported players, Colin McCool and myself from Australia and Peter Wight from the West Indies managed to score more than 1,000 runs in the season. Between us we scored almost half the county's runs.

I was up and down the batting order like a yo-yo. I started the season opening with Yorkshireman Lou Pickles, but gradually dropped down the order. Once I even batted at No. 8, before climbing back up and finishing the season as the regular opening batsman.

What a, season! Somerset cricket in 1958 certainly wasn't a game for the faint-hearted or the nervous. It was nearly all

X-certificate stuff that would have done credit for Alfred Hitchcock.

We managed to sneak home in one match by 11 runs after looking completely out of the running. Picked up another 14 points victory by only eight runs and then, a month later, scraped home by only four runs. That was the season we dropped first innings points to Middlesex in a rain-ruined match by only three runs after needing only six runs for the lead with six wickets intact. It was thrill-a-minute cricket all the way.

We started these capers early in May against Essex at Ilford. We had not played a game in Somerset by then, although it was our third match of the season. The weather was more suited to Winter Olympics than cricket when Maurice Tremlett won the toss and decided to bat. The boys were grateful. At least they could keep in the warmth of the dressing-room!

Not for long though. Apart from Peter Wight, who scored 69, the rest of us did not stay around for long out in the cold. We were all out for 188 and any hope we had of picking up points had disappeared by tea on the second day when Essex's first innings plodded to a close. We were 154 runs behind.

Peter soon changed that on the third day, when play started after lunch following rain which had washed out the first two hours. With help from Colin McCool and Geoff Lomax, Peter steered us to 312 for four by tea on the last day. Peter was unbeaten on 130.

That left Essex chasing 159 runs to win in 115 minutes and again the match looked like going their way as Dickie Dodds and Gordon Barker lashed the first 50 runs in only eighteen minutes. Then, Brian Langford moved into the picture with his off-spinners.

Essex tried to hit him out of sight . . . but failed. We took our catches and had a bit of luck when Doug Insole, one player who might have swept Essex to victory with his unorthodox style, moved into a delivery from fast bowler Brian Lobb and had to go off with a head injury. Doug came back at the fall of the ninth wicket but became Langford's eighth victim in their second innings and we were home by 11 runs with fifteen minutes to spare.

That was only the start of our nerve-racking moments to

come that summer. The next one came a fortnight later when Robin Marlar, the Sussex skipper, declared 98 runs behind on the first innings of a rain-interrupted match at Taunton in order to make a game of it.

Once again we had batted first with Wight scoring another century in our first innings of 345. Sussex looked capable of matching that when they had scored 247 for three by lunch on the third day. Then Marlar declared with Jim Parks only eight short of his 'ton'.

Maurice took up the challenge to fight to the death. We went after runs quickly, lost wickets even more quickly and had added only 65 for six when Maurice declared leaving Sussex 164 runs to get in 115 minutes.

It was a sporting decision by Maurice, because Lobb had been injured in his first innings bowling stint and this left us a fast bowler short. Maurice threw the 'cherry' to me and in my first over I took two wickets and sent back Les Lenham, Don Smith, Alan Oakman and Jim Parks by the time Sussex had scored 55 for four.

Everything was going our way until Ian Thomson, Sussex's medium-pace bowler, came to the wicket and started lashing us around. From 97 for seven he took Sussex to 153, only 11 runs short of victory, when he played over the top of a delivery from Geoff Lomax. The last two wickets added only another two runs and this time there was only four minutes left of extra time when we clinched the match.

The next time we went into extra time was a month later, against Derbyshire at Bath.

Maurice Tremlett and I had shared in a 104 fifth wicket partnership in 80 minutes on the first day to boost Somerset to 236. Derbyshire were struggling from the first ball when Les Hamer was bowled by Bryan Webb. Only George Dawkes batted with any confidence and they were bowled out for 169. If they were bad, we were worse in our second innings against the bowling of Cliff Gladwin, who took seven for 59.

He put Derbyshire right in the game for the first time since the match started. They were left needing 188 to win in 243 minutes. Conditions were a little tricky after a heavy thunderstorm early in the morning, but time was on their side.

I

That was when the fun started. The match swung our way
when they lost their first four wickets for only 33 runs . . . and
then right back in Derbyshire's direction as skipper Donald
Carr, now assistant secretary at Lord's, and Laurie Johnson
put on 116 for the fifth wicket.

Eric Bryant, a slow left-arm bowler from Weston-super-
Mare, dismissed them both and started a minor collapse. The
next four wickets went for only one run before we were once
more jolted out of our victory mood.

From 150 for eight with 38 runs needed for victory Edwin
Smith and Cliff Gladwin slowly inched Derbyshire towards the
target. Still together when Maurice claimed the extra half an
hour, they looked like snatching a dramatic victory. The new
ball saved us.

Peter Wight picked up Smith off Geoff Lomax's bowling with
the score at 178 and five runs later – with Derbyshire still needing five runs to win – Geoff found the edge of Gladwin's bat and
I snaffled up the chance. These were situations to test nerves
of any hard bitten professional.

That was the end of our nail-biting finishes, but not the finish
of some strange matches that season.

The strangest of all was against Lancashire at Weston-super-
Mare – which must go down as Brian Langford's match – on a
wicket which gave the bowlers all the help they needed right
from the first day when only 110 minutes play was possible.

Brian Statham and Roy Tattersall quickly rolled us over for
only 60 runs in Somerset's first innings, each finishing with five
wickets apiece.

Our innings had been an almost continuous procession of
batsmen walking to the wicket and out again. Lancashire's
went the same way against Langford's off-spin. Nine of them
went his way in a career best performance costing him only 26
runs in 13 overs.

Despite Langford's bowling, Lancashire still held a first
innings lead of 29, a healthy-looking total when we started
batting a second time.

We had lost six wickets for 57 in no time when Ken Palmer
joined Dennis Silk. Both batted magnificently on a turning
wicket. Dennis finished with 77 in their 100-minute 112-run

partnership, including four sixes and eight fours as he tucked into the bowling of Malcolm Hilton.

They were match-winning performances as Somerset's second innings grew to 177 leaving Lancashire without a chance on that wicket. But even allowing for the state of the wicket Lancashire batted badly. They were bowled out for 59 in exactly 100 minutes with not one of the Lancashire batsmen reaching double figures. Langford finished with six for 28, match figures of 15 for 54. Altogether he took 35 wickets for 279 runs in the three match Weston-super-Mare festival.

Those were the matches we won. Now for the one we should have won, but lost – to Yorkshire.

This was another up-and-downer at Bath. Half our first innings was over before we really got started. In fact, we lost our first seven wickets for only 85 with a fellow called Trueman doing most of the damage before Geoff Lomax went in and scored a great unbeaten 94 before running out of partners.

Geoff's innings took Somerset to 274, exactly 102 more than Yorkshire managed when they batted. Only Frank Lowson showed any confidence with a half century as the Yorkshire innings folded. It left us holding all the cards. But not for long.

There was not much time left for play on the second day when we started our second innings. The stormclouds were gathering, the light was poor and Fred Trueman took full advantage. Before the close, he had skittled three of us out for only 14 runs.

This was another of our many batting failures that summer. Only opening bat, Lou Pickles, a Yorkshireman, with 18 and myself with 20 reached double figures in the second innings as we were shot out for 65. Yorkshire had little trouble scoring the 168 for victory for the loss of three wickets. It was a match Somerset should have won. If we had, we might also have won the County championship for the first time.

That 1958 was a strange summer considering the number of low scores we made and the high position we finished in the County table. We might even have established a peculiar record. Each wicket we took cost us two runs more than we scored for each wicket we lost!

TWENTY

'Keep running, lad'

Old Alec Skelding was the model umpire, a chap after my own heart. He knew exactly the right time to put the chatter in, like one of those old-time music-hall comedians who had us rolling in the aisles.

He was standing in one particular game at Lord's when we needed about half-a-dozen runs with six wickets left. The ground had been under water after a downpour and it was so black you could hardly see.

Nevertheless, we were all anxious to win the thirty shillings bonus for first innings lead and the Middlesex skipper, John Warr, a great lad and sportsman, said: 'We'll go out and field if you are game enough to bat.'

The general feeling in the Somerset dressing-room was that we needed only about five minutes to knock off the runs. Our skipper, Harold Stephenson, looked up at the mass of angry clouds and told me, as a left-hander, to bat lower down to save any time-wasting.

We lost two quick wickets and Harold went in and had a whack. I was next man in and waiting near the gates as the skipper took a tremendous swing and was caught magnificently, one-handed on the boundary edge.

Chris Greetham, a very strong hitter of the ball, was still there, but Middlesex, by now, were right in the hunt themselves for first innings lead. They were just as keen as us and, remember, we hadn't scored a run while losing three wickets.

Chris smashed the next ball through the covers – he hit it like a bomb – but I thought to myself it wouldn't get through all the mud and slosh. We'd better settle for three. So we took off to run, and Old Alec Skelding was umpiring at square-leg. I got about half-way down the wicket when I saw something red or black pass me. It was the ball – and John Murray was coming rapidly up to the stumps. By this time I was three-parts down the wicket and Alec was walking in, raising his finger and saying in the same breath: 'Keep running, lad, you'll never make it.' I kept on running – to the pavilion. I was out by yards.

We never did get those six runs. But it was a fabulous game and I can still see old Alec in his white sandshoes, walking towards me, with his finger raised.

Alec was a great character. It was a pity he passed on. Everyone would have accepted him as an umpire until he was 100.

He had this marvellous sense of fun and people used to look forward to a little bit of comic business at the end of an over. These sort of antics are frowned on nowadays, and I know from good authority that one or two umpires have been told that their job is to control the game and not chat with the players. My own view is that if a man is a talker out in the middle, he either makes it as an umpire or he doesn't.

I was the younger generation to Alec, and I can remember him standing in another match against Surrey at Weston. Peter May played the ball around square to me twenty yards away. I dived, caught it very close to the ground, and rolled over. Peter didn't budge. We had to make a double appeal and Alec raised a very angry finger and pointed down the wicket to Peter. 'That's out!' he said.

Peter then left the wicket, and Alec had a word with him as he walked back to the pavilion. I often wonder what he said.

I've taken a few umpires for a ride in my time, but I remember one game against Warwickshire when 'Dusty' Rhodes, a great friend of mine, outsmarted me in an argument. It was getting close to stumps and we were pressing for an early wicket, after declaring at a big total. We finished one over and dashed to the other end to get in another.

'Dusty' walked slowly up to the wicket, pulled up the stumps and had a bit of a laugh to himself. Everyone said: 'Bloody hell, Dusty! There are two minutes left yet.'

He insisted that it was time, but we were blazing mad because we were confident of getting a wicket in the last over. Afterwards in the bar 'Dusty' turned to me and asked: 'Were you angry out there – about me pulling up the stumps?'

I replied: 'I was bloody fair dinkum and if I were captain, I'd slate you on the spot.'

Next morning when we went out to take up our positions 'Dusty' and I didn't say a word to each other. Usually I would walk up and say: 'Good morning, ump' and blow my nose on his coat – or something like that.

Kenny Palmer took a wicket in the first over and I walked over from my position in the gully to pick up a stump. 'Dusty' walked in from square-leg – he was wearing a nice pair of suede shoes. He didn't look at me as I pretended to throw the stump at him. He just muttered: 'None of your bloody Australian ways here.'

The ground was a bit soft early in the morning – the hole for the wicket was too big – and Dusty put his foot there to stamp the hole smaller for the stump. I went to put the stump in the hole and accidentally almost pierced Dusty's suede shoe! I saw my mistake straightaway and said: 'I'm sorry, Dusty. I didn't mean to do that.'

He said: 'Oh, don't worry about it. I have got a dozen more pairs of shoes at home.' We never looked at each other and never spoke a word right through that day!

I remember another game, many years back, when I first started playing for Somerset. This match was at Lord's and I was opening the bowling against a Middlesex line-up which included Denis Compton, Bill Edrich and Jack Robertson.

Frank Lee, who was reckoned by many people as the No. 1 umpire, was standing in this match. I had just had Compton caught for a 'duck' and Edrich came in to join Robertson. I bowled Jack a couple of outers and he went across and played them as a proper stroke player does. Then I bowled one that came back at him and Jack didn't get across quite enough. Well, Harold Stephenson and I and first slip all roared for leg-before.

We had our backs up after getting rid of Compton for a duck.

Old Frank said quietly: 'Not out.' At the end of the over he turned to me and said: 'Missed the leg stump by an inch.' Well, I blew up. I told him: 'As far as I'm concerned, Frank, I hope I never see you in Somerset again!' But, in my heart, I knew Frank was right.

I didn't see Frank for a long time after this incident and our next meeting was at a Hastings Festival game. I was bowling again, and I threw one up short on the leg-side for Tony Lock to hit. Of course, 'Lockie' whacked it and the ball sailed out of the ground towards the sea. They were a long time retrieving it and when it did come back I gestured to the crowd that it had been in the 'drink'. For a joke I stepped over to Frank and started to rub the ball on his white coat to dry it off.

This was great fun for the crowd. But it wasn't for Frank. He pulled away in disgust and said: 'There are members of the MCC here and they might report me for this sort of thing.'

I said: 'Don't be bloody silly. This is a festival match not a bloody Test match.'

Yet it might have been a Test match as far as Frank was concerned. He was strict right up to the day he finished. I admired his conscientiousness, but sometimes I think he could have relaxed a little more, especially at these 'end of term' games.

I always told Ron Lay, a man who never played first-class cricket but who became one of our finest umpires, that he would have a place in my book, if ever I wrote one. And here's my chance to honour that promise.

This is the story of the 'crooked line'. The game was at Rushden and this business concerned Frank Tyson and Mickey Norman.

Northampton had bowled first and Frank had made a terrible hole across the popping crease. This happened at a time when Harold Stephenson and I were getting them stumped down the leg-side. I pitched the ball well up, more or less right on the popping crease line. The batsman played forward and over the top, dragged his back foot and 'Steve' did the rest. I used to get several wickets every season in this way. 'Steve' was such a brilliant 'keeper on the leg-side, he knew when I was going to bowl that particular ball and it was no trouble to him to pick it up.

Ron Lay was umpiring at square-leg, and I thought this was the right time to do the job. I pitched it perfectly. Mickey Norman played forward and Steve whipped off the bails. I looked towards square-leg and Ron walked in to put the bails back. He grinned and said: 'Not out! '

Mickey was still out of his crease and 'Steve' knocked the three stumps nearly out of the ground. 'Well, that must be bloody out,' he appealed to Ron.

Ron still walked in, chewing a toffee and grinning his head off. 'Not out! ' he repeated.

'Steve' asked: 'Well, why isn't he out?' and Ron replied: 'The line's crooked. I couldn't see.'

We thought Ron was being stupid, but when we cooled down we saw his point. Ron was standing twenty-yards back at square-leg. There was this hole of about four inches and he couldn't see the line.

Ron was a very good umpire and he was right to give the batsman the benefit of the doubt. It is a great loss to the game that Ron has decided to quit and I'm personally sorry he is not around to show me the ropes now that I am in the hot-seat.

It's not going to be easy taking up umpiring after being an umpire baiter for over 30 years. But I hope I can benefit from the lessons I've learned as a player. I have no illusions about my new job. It must be a very hard thing to keep your concentration as an umpire over a full day. You have so many points to consider and you're completely on your own.

Many top-class players couldn't stand the strain. People like Eddie Paynter – he would often advise a bowler how to dismiss a particular batsman – and Winston Place and Freddie Gardner used to take it too much to heart.

Difficult decisions would prey on their minds, and a cursing from ungracious batsmen didn't help their insomnia. I've seldom met a player who thought he was out, even if all three were knocked down. And, of course, Eddie and Winston knew all about these pavilion tantrums. They'd gone through it themselves as players.

I can sympathise with their problems, but I've got few

Left: I've bowled a few
overs since this picture was
taken in 1957. *Below:* Still
hitting 'em, in one of my
last games for Somerset, *v*
Sussex, August 1968. Jim
Parks is behind the stumps

Left: Lambing time in Somerset. The author with two new recruits

Below: More new arrivals under the inspection of myself and my wife Betty

worries about the job. Old rivalries with players will have to be wiped out. As a professional umpire, I cannot get involved too much with players.

Since my appointment to the umpires' list people have asked: 'What is going to happen if you pick up Somerset in your first year. Suppose you get an appeal against them for leg-before?'

My reply is that I will give all ten batsmen out leg-before if I think I'm right. It will not make any difference which team is batting. I shall make my decisions without fear or favour.

Eddie Paynter was a great talker as player and umpire on the cricket field. I'm not far behind him as a chatterbox but now I shall have to learn to control myself. I cannot tell the batsman what the ball is doing and the best way to deal with a particular bowler.

I can see it *is* going to be a very lonely life. You can have the occasional word with a player, but you risk a break in your concentration if you start a real conversation. You could be reduced to just counting the six balls – and there's a lot more to umpiring than that. From what I can see, as a new boy, it is a bigger task for an umpire to stand for six hours than it is for a batsman to score a 100.

During my playing days I often got hot under the collar as a victim of leg-before decisions, but I can truthfully say that as a batsman I always accepted the umpire's verdict.

I used to pride myself on being a good 'walker'. In fact, I've even given myself out before the bowler appealed. Somerset were playing Lancashire and the bowler was Brian Statham. The ball thumped my pads and immediately I set off for the dressing-room. Geoff Clayton, the 'keeper, who later joined us in Somerset, called out: 'Don't go, Bill. The ump's given you "not out".'

'I couldn't care less,' I shouted back. 'That ball would have knocked all three stumps out.'

It was my tribute to the accuracy of Statham, the straightest bowler in the game. It seemed to me that, if you missed him with the bat, you must be either leg-before or bowled.

Of course, there have been times when I've ticked myself off for 'walking' on appeal. I recall one game at Leicester when I set off for the pavilion after a loud appeal for a catch behind the wicket. As I passed Maurice Hallam, the Leicestershire captain, I told him: 'You know I never played that bloody ball, Maurice.' He replied: 'Then what the hell are you "walking" for?'

I realised that I had never hit the ball, but 'walking' on appeal was an automatic reaction. I had given myself out and I shall never know whether the umpire would have agreed with me. He most likely thought to himself: 'Well, he's a good "walker", this feller.'

Speaking as a player, I would say that you should always walk on appeal, but in my new role as umpire I would prefer that the batsman left the decision to me.

Sometimes you might get a situation where the batsman slightly nicks the ball. The wicket-keeper is unsure whether it was bat or pad and he relies on the umpire.

This business of 'walking' is a very debatable question. My fellow Aussies never walk on principle. There are English Test players who won't budge either, and I've always found the top-class player 'walks' less than the average county batsman.

It is difficult to reach a firm conclusion on the rights and wrongs of 'walking'. So much depends on the personality of the player but, for the record, I would have no hesitation in calling back the player who 'walks' if I thought he was not out. This does not mean that a batsman cannot give himself out. I remember one game at Taunton when a Somerset batsman, who was never a great lover of fast bowling, was under fire from Frank Tyson. Frank was really making the ball fly around and the batsman didn't need a second bidding after a muttered appeal for a catch behind the wicket. You couldn't really blame him with the 'Typhoon' in such a mood. The batsman at the other end told him he wasn't within a foot of the ball and the fieldsmen said: 'What are you walking for?'

The answer came: 'Oh, I hit the camber off it' – and he buzzed off to the pavilion.

As an umpire, I shall have to be careful not to show any bias in favour of the batsman or the bowler. But you cannot get away from the fact that the fast bowler has been the whipping-boy over the last ten years. He hasn't been given any advantage over the batsman.

The legislators have tried for years to kill the toiling seamer. They've cut down his approach to the wicket and any chap with a bit of speed has been accused of throwing.

When throwing became a controversy and was written up in the papers, there were some players who welcomed the chance to put a bowler out of the game.

I remember once having a glass of milk with the Yorkshire boys. I said that there was a lot of squealing going on about the Australians, O'Rourke and Meckiff. One Yorkshireman turned to me and said: 'Bill, we're the first to squeal when someone throws faster than us!'

Personally, I think it is a very hard thing to call a player for throwing. You can ruin his career and rob him of a benefit of five or six thousand pounds. The cruel irony of this business is that one umpire might say the bowler throws and the rest of the umpires don't call him.

Spotting the thrower is one of the most difficult decisions in cricket. Many players are convinced that Harold Rhodes of Derbyshire throws. Now I have opened up against Harold and I don't mind telling you he was ruddy quick. But I've always said, in my opinion, that he didn't throw.

On a private tour of Pakistan arranged by Ron Roberts, Charlie Griffith joined us soon after the controversy which surrounded him in England.

In Pakistan the batsmen had more time to pick the ball up in the lighter atmosphere and Charlie was unable to pitch his yorker which they said he threw in England. The ball seemed to come through more as a full toss and the batsmen had only to push forward on the hard grounds and it was fourpennyworth.

I have my doubts as to whether Charlie actually threw – people said it was the quicker ball he chucked and beat the English batsmen because they couldn't pick it up quickly enough.

You could say that his action was controversial – front-on delivery and foot well outside – but I never saw him bowl a ball which I reckoned he threw. In Pakistan, he was trying to play cricket and scuttle them with his fast yorker.

Quite honestly, as an umpire, I don't think you can be quick enough to judge whether a bowler throws or not. But fortunately for my peace of mind there is no-one currently playing in English county cricket to bother me on that score.

The television snoopers, the former Test players making their comments in their little box high above the wicket will be a bigger worry.

I remember talking to Syd Buller, following the controversy involving young Keith Fletcher in the Leeds Test last year. Syd judged that Keith had tickled the ball down the leg side for a catch behind the wicket, and he gave him out.

Syd accused television commentators of making snap judgments from 200 yards away and saying that the umpire was wrong. He was plainly annoyed that the television critics could go out on a limb and say that the ball had moved just away from the bat after travelling down the wicket at between seventy and eighty miles-per-hour.

He reckoned in the future umpires would only be concerned with counting six balls an over. If there was a leg-before appeal, a red or green light would flash on in the box to indicate the decision.

Television playbacks may provide the soccer and cricket commentators with talking points, but it is making life difficult for the legion of umpires and referees who are paid to do their jobs to the best of their ability. And it's a hell of a thing when you get the commentators condemning these fellows. It's time some of these former Test-players-turned-broadcasters stopped undermining the umpire's authority. Their best service to the game which made them would be to back umpires – or shut up.

As an umpire I am, of course, concerned about those colleagues in the West Indies who face intimidation because they are brave enough to give honest decisions. But I must say, the best man should be appointed to umpire in a Test match. Appointing a neutral umpire to guard against bitterness doesn't really solve the matter. It is the standard of umpiring which is all important.

This is my aim now – to measure up to the highest standards. I shall not rest content until I have umpired in a Test match, and all my energies will be devoted to convincing the MCC and the county captains that I am the man to do the job. It would be a happy finale to my cricketing career.

TWENTY ONE

The Country gentleman

Three cheers for the landed gentry of Somerset!

I'm not one of them myself, mind you, but just to walk around my two-acre smallholding near Taunton makes me glow with pride. It's nice to feel that I've got a stake in this beautiful county. My wife and I and our two boys, Timothy and Douglas, live very happily in our little country retreat just outside Taunton.

I'll never forget the day I bought this piece of land. I agreed terms with the owner and bragged: 'As a matter of fact, I'll pay you cash. Let's shake hands on it, gentlemen's agreement, and we'll see the solicitors in the morning.'

'Well,' he said. 'We'd better have a drink on that. Do you drink cider?' I replied: 'Well, just in a little way.' And he went off to get a bottle. He disappeared inside a dark room and I heard bottles clinking. Finally he emerged with a bottle which was covered in dust. He poured me out a glass. The liquid was green.

I smiled at him – it was more of a grimace actually – and I thought to myself: 'Hell! I'll have to drink this.' As it rumbled down my throat I could feel it tearing my tonsils out.

No sooner had I polished that drink off than this feller said: 'There's some more here, you can have.' I winced. 'I'll be

141

doing myself an injustice if I go on swigging this,' I replied.

Undeterred, he gave me another glass of this green stuff and I managed to force it down.

Not long afterwards I was driving home through the lanes in my van, and all the time the hedges on either side of the road seemed to be getting closer. I thought I would never succeed in getting the van up the driveway when I got home, but I just squeezed into the garage. When I staggered in my wife said: 'You haven't been to buy the ground – you've been to the pub. Look at your eyes. You're three-parts drunk.'

She was right! I'd only had two glasses of cider. But, blimey, it was so rough it was rotting my socks.

They used to make hundreds of gallons of cider round here. One chap, who lived just across the road from me, would put up two or three barrels for himself and buy some more at a local auction. Both he and his wife were over eighty. I used to tell his missus: 'Now, you want to watch him tonight. He's got that glitter in his eye.' I'd tell the husband: 'Now off you go, straight to bed.' And he would say: 'Not until I've had a couple of pints of cider.'

I keep a few sheep to crop the grass. At one time we had a few hundred head of poultry, but I reckoned it wasn't fair to expect my wife to run things, especially when I started to play cricket seven days a week. Anyway, there was no money in it and the price of eggs started to go down. I thought that rather than work for the food firms I would sell the poultry.

I've never made cider myself, but we used to shake a few tons of apples from our trees and take them to the cider company. Over the years the crop has got smaller, but I can remember returning from one overseas tour and finding apples all over the place. We phoned the cider company and told them we had plenty of apples but they would have to come and pick them. They agreed to do this, but when they came out they found thistles and grass four feet high. They weren't too pleased. Just imagine trying to shake the apples down among the nettles. They never came again!

I play the role of the country gentleman down here in Somerset. I follow the Quantock Hunt, under the Mastership of Mr P. Rolffe-Sylvester, and we meet to go stag hunting at Triscombe, Deadwoman's Ditch, Bagborough and the Traveller's Rest, and hunt all over the Quantock Hills.

A feller with whom I used to skittle in Bridgwater, Dennis Cavill, introduced me to stag hunting. On our first two or three outings I would say: 'There go the dogs.' Now this is the worst thing you can say on a Hunt, but I've learned the rules of the sport now. I use my authority a bit and stand on my dignity when the uninitiated say: 'Are the dogs running across there?' I get very stern and tell them: 'Not the dogs, love, the HOUNDS.'

Many people, particularly in schools, have got the wrong idea about stag-hunting. They think that the hounds catch the stag and just rip it to pieces. It's never been drummed into them, as it has with the country folk, what actually goes on at a Hunt.

The lads and lasses go on their nature study lessons from the schools in Taunton. They say: 'There are those dogs tearing those poor things to pieces again.' They haven't got a clue because it has never been explained to them at school.

From the time they start hunting the hounds learn to pick up the scent. They can break off six or seven times on different stags or hinds, but if they are hunting one stag, it might be five or six hours before they run him down. Nine times out of ten the stag runs into the bracken or some other shelter and the scent is lost. He just stands there and the Master gets off his horse and shoots the stag dead behind the ear. He allows the hounds to smell the stag. Then he gives the word of command and the hounds back away – they don't even try to touch it.

The Master will then carve up the stag and hand out the liver and kidneys to whoever is around. The heart generally goes to the farmer on whose ground the stag has been killed. But you cannot convince people that this sport isn't cruel. Some days go by when we don't kill at all. You can be up there five hours and lose the stag completely. He might dive into a batch of five or six hinds and away they'll run in all directions. Some of the hounds will go here, some will go there, and before you know where you are the hounds have all disappeared. They've gone off on different scents.

The appeal of stag hunting for me is the way the hounds behave and the pattern of the chase. There are days when we've been out for about four hours and the Master knows we have lost the stag. He doesn't know whether to go back and start again and he might have lost half his hounds. I'll joke to the Master: 'Well, they're exercising the stag again today. We've come to give him a bit of exercise.'

You can take my word that I would be against this sport if I saw the stag being cornered and torn to pieces.

Fox-hunting is a different business altogether. I remember watching a fox-hunt at Berkeley in Gloucestershire. The hounds pulled this fox to pieces and all they recovered was the tail, or the brush as they call it. This was cruel as far as I'm concerned.

On the stag hunt they stop as soon as the animal is cornered. They don't go any further. The Master comes in and immediately shoots the stag. One shot, bang, and down he drops.

I once took Frank Tyson fishing on the reservoir at Durley. We had started the match on the Saturday and I got permission from the owner to take a boat out on the reservoir on the Sunday. It was a really hot day and before long Frank was looking just like a boiled lobster. I could see him getting redder and redder. Somerset were resuming against Northampton the next day, and I thought to myself the more sun he gets the slower he'll be when he starts to bowl against us!

Frank was a novice as a fisherman and I told him to take it steady and see if he could cast between some weeds at the end of the reservoir. All of a sudden Frank felt a tug at the line and he thought he had a bulldozer at the other end.

I urged Frank to let the rod do the work. I appealed to him to hold the rod there with one hand and not to fight the fish. 'Take it gently and just have a go at him now and again,' I said.

Well, Frank was a bit too impatient. I suppose he was excited at the prospect of landing his first fish. 'Let's get the bugger in,' he said. He yelled: 'Let's get him in! '

By this time he was standing in the boat and winding away like fury. Eventually I saw the fish. It was a beauty, a brown trout. Frank saw it, too, and shouted for me to haul it in with the landing net.

I wouldn't allow Frank to use the landing net. I said: 'Don't show him anything. Let him play around a bit.'

You could see the fish under the water, and Frank had pulled it almost into the boat. I'm convinced that in another five minutes he would have brought him in nicely and put the net under him. Frank was fishing on very light gear and I thought to myself: 'He'll lose the blighter when it gets a bit nearer. He'll bloody go.' Frank kept on moaning and groaning about the net. He lifted the trout out of the water and reached down for the net.

Then the fish saw the net and it dived away back into the water. Frank just stood there with the rod in his hand. He couldn't believe what had happened. I gently explained that the art of fishing lay in coaxing the fish to its doom. 'All you were concerned about was getting the fish into the boat. You could have had the time of your life playing that feller and he would have killed himself and just floated up.'

Next morning Frank could hardly move when he arrived at the cricket ground. Fortunately Northampton were batting and he didn't have to bowl until later in the afternoon. Poor Frank! He really suffered on that fishing expedition. I wonder if he still talks about the one that got away. . . .

After chuckling at Frank's misfortune, I think perhaps I'd better end this chapter with a story against myself. This was the time I got seasick. I've travelled all over the world in planes and ships, but this happened on a sea trip near my home in Somerset. I always used to take pride in being a good sailor until I went fishing about ten miles out in a small boat last year and brought up my bootlaces. I was hellish sick. We had taken a load of grog, whisky, gin and cider and sandwiches. And I never ate a thing all day. I haven't been out since. I seem to have lost my confidence. I daren't go out in a boat again in case my tummy wobbles and spoils a day's fishing.

K

TWENTY TWO

Sacked by Somerset

I suppose the only way that 'getting the sack' is not too painful is when it comes with a 'Golden' handshake. Too often, in cricket, there is not so much as a gentle wave of the hand when it is time for goodbye.

It makes me particularly sad that Somerset have, in my opinion, failed to strike the right note when discarding some players. I must admit right away that I was hurt as much by the way Somerset finished with me as I was by being forced to give up the championship game.

I say 'forced' because at my age it was never likely that another club would offer me a contract under the terms required by special registration. I could have played for another county only if I achieved a residential qualification or by Special Registration.

By the time I achieved residential status I might really have begun to look my age! I think that Somerset would have raised no objection to my being specially registered with another club, but my new county would have been required by the terms of the Special Registration to sign me for a minimum of three years.

I feel fit enough to play for another ten years, but it is a bit much to expect a new county committee to commit themselves to a player of my age for a minimum three years period.

Surely it was different for Somerset. I had been playing for the club for twelve years and although I was not turning in the same performances as I did in my prime, there was nobody in the side with better all-round figures, season by season. Very few players in the whole championship did their averages much good during 1968. It was one of those years when the weather spoilt so many games.

I think that most of us were glad when it was over and we said a prayer that we would have the sun on our backs next season.

I was never so shaken in my life as when the note came through the door offering me terms for only Gillette matches and Sunday cricket in 1969. And I was damned annoyed when within seconds the newspapers were on the telephone asking me what I was going to do now! They must have got the news before I did.

The way things get into the newspapers is often mysterious but I was angry that I had been caught on the hop. My pride was hurt because I had been sacked and to get my notice in a letter through the post was a bit harsh in my opinion.

I drove into Taunton to see Richard Robinson the County secretary. He said: 'Well, Bill, that is the way the Committee want it. They would like you to play in the Sunday games and any Gillette cup matches but they don't feel they can renew your contract for championship cricket.'

Apparently the Committee had decided on a 'youth' policy. The first thing was to reduce the age limit. Who can argue that on this score they had to start with me! I will argue, however, that it could not be a good cricket decision because I believe there just wasn't a reserve of youngsters to move into the first-class fixtures.

A few days later I went to see Richard Robinson again. I was not sure that the Committee realised that I wanted to accommodate them if at all possible, so far as a contract was concerned.

Obviously, too, I was anxious to stay in the game if I could because I enjoyed it so much and knew I was fit enough to carry on. I stressed to Richard Robinson that I would accept match fees for championship games. This would commit the Committee to very little. If I was not fit or not good enough I would not be chosen and therefore would not be paid. It was a gamble I was prepared to take because I did not think I would be out of work very often. In my twelve years with Somerset I think I missed only two games.

I asked the Somerset Secretary if he could make sure that the Committee understood this and that I was prepared to go on playing without a contract.

If I could get the Committee to change their minds and retain me on a match-by-match basis I was prepared to take whatever came. If, however, the Committee confirmed that they did not want me, I had to start looking around for something else.

I could not accept the offer to play Sunday games only because at the most, if I had played in all games, I would have received only about £300. Even if Somerset again reached the final of the Gillette cup there would not be much extra in it for me.

I needed a better income than that because even though I am not short of a bob or two I have two lads still at school and living gets dearer not cheaper.

I was determined to stay in cricket if at all possible and I reckoned that if I could not play first-class cricket the next best thing would be to apply to go on the first-class umpire's list. The closing date for applications for the 1969 Season was very near and I asked Richard Robinson if he could get a decision from the Somerset Committee fairly quickly. He said he would try to get a quorum of members together.

Later he told me that a date which had been chosen for a meeting was not now suitable and another date would have to be arranged. I could not afford to wait longer because I would miss the Umpire's application date. Also, the Somerset Secretary thought it unlikely that the meeting, when it was arranged, would want to change the general policy of concentrating on youth. I felt it was pointless to hang on and telephoned to Lord's for an Umpire's application form.

Now that my playing days with Somerset are over my big regret is that the happy memories of playing with the team all over the country are somewhat soured by the manner of my leaving. I saw other players who appeared to be affected in much

the same way, just for the want, as I see it, of a little awareness
of the feelings of a cricketer when he is not wanted any more.
I do not, of course, mean that Somerset players have been cast
aside and deliberately ignored.

Perhaps the best way I can put it is that the instinctive warmth
and friendliness which Somerset cricket has always shared with
crowds on the field is not always so evident, in my experience,
in the relationship between the playing staff and administration.

Perhaps it is inevitable in a rural county where the com-
mitteemen and players not only live far apart and therefore
seldom meet, but also have little in common either in being
Somerset born or speaking with the same accent or dialect!

Maybe when the Committee decided to call it a day so far as
I was concerned, they reasoned . . . 'Well, we can't expect the
old boy to go on for ever. He's had a damned good run and
we have been lucky to have him. It's a pity, we shall miss him,
but if he can play on Sundays that will do him and us a bit of
good.'

That is the way they might have thought it out, but it did
not reach me that way. It is quite tragic – the lack of com-
munication that can exist between the Club and players at times.
No player, so far as I know, has any reason to complain about
the relationship while actually playing, but when the time
comes to part, it has sometimes been a clumsy process.

Somerset did ask me to join them. The first time I was in the
middle of a contract with Blackpool and there was nothing I
could do about it even if I wanted to do so. At that time I did
not want to leave Blackpool, but Somerset kept at me for the
next two years and when the time came for me to renew with
Blackpool, Somerset again asked me to give up the league and
join them.

I was treated very well for most of the time. The only time I
felt badly treated was over the captaincy business. The way I
was eventually 'sacked' was completely different from the welcome from the Committee when I arrived in the county.

Other players to my knowledge have been equally hurt by the
manner in which they have departed. One of the greatest ever
to play for Somerset, the incomparable Arthur Wellard, who
was on the staff for over twenty-five years, was so upset that he

did not return to watch a match in Somerset for eighteen years. He went back then, in 1968, only because his old pal and bowling partner, Bill Andrews, who lives in Weston-super-Mare, suggested that the sea air would be ideal for Mrs Wellard to convalesce after an illness. Arthur went to stay with Bill and was given a tremendous reception by the crowd when he strolled into the ground to watch a Festival match. Arthur admitted then, and has told me since, the reason he stayed away from Somerset so long.

Arthur, realising that his playing days were closing down, and hearing that the Club was looking for a coach, applied for the job. Arthur recalls 'They told me I would never make a coach. Then, at the end of the season, they told me they would not want me next year. That hurt a lot. I could, I think, have been given more notice. Some time later they came to London and asked me to take the coaching job, but I was not prepared to risk the same treatment again.'

Arthur always turns up to see us when we are at Lord's. He, too, was in his fiftieth year when Somerset finished with him and I swear there isn't now a fitter 67-year-old anywhere. The man who was told he would 'never make a coach' is a full-time coach at the Middlesex indoor school, at Finchley, and still plays in local club and schools matches!

I can honestly say that during my years with Somerset I rarely saw a former professional player at any of our home games. There is something very sad about the apathetic drifting away of characters and personalities who could continue to stimulate goodwill for the Club.

It was four months after I had been told that I was not required for championship cricket again when I received a very pleasant letter from the Chairman, Mr E. F. Longrigg, extending the Committee's invitation that I should become an Honorary Life Member for my services to Somerset cricket and cricket entertainment. It was a gesture usually made to professionals with fair services to the Club and I was pleased to receive it, but it left me mystified. Such a gesture, given sooner, would have taken the pain from the sacking.

The Committee does indeed know how to say 'Thank You'. Colin Atkinson, who was released from teaching duties at

Millfield School by Mr R. J. O. Meyer, his headmaster, so that
he could captain Somerset, was presented with a silver salver
when he packed in.

In contrast there was the case of Maurice Tremlett.

Tremlett, a player with staggering natural talent, allowed
himself to be pressured by forces who insisted that he should
change his style. Despite two MCC tours, he lost his confidence
but, with real guts, applied himself to batting and straightaway
broke the Somerset aggregate record.

Then, when a fearful blow above the eye in a match at Bath,
where he was fielding at silly mid-off, nearly cost him his life, he
showed more courage in staying in the game.

He suffered agony trying to get used to wearing spectacles
and contact lenses and eventually recovered some form.

Often, however, he was 'playing from memory' but he was
still better than most. When he was appointed the first professional captain of the county he brilliantly led the side to third
position, in 1958, the highest in the Club's history since the
championship assumed its present form.

It was obvious, however, that he could not continue for long
and, when a good business offer turned up, he accepted it.
When he left, he was not, as far as I know, even elected to life
membership, an honour which had been given to other players
of distinction.

His new job took him to Hampshire and, within hours, he
received an invitation to be a Life Member of the county club
and to use the ground facilities whenever he wished!

Every evening in the summer he can be seen in the nets
bowling to his two sons and any other lad who likes to turn up.
Both sons have a natural talent. Is there any doubt in which
county it will flower, if it does indeed blossom?

The sad thing about cricket today is that on the field we
miss the gay, uninhibited skills of the good amateurs while
there is too much old school tie nonsense behind the scenes.
Cricket today is big business, but business in which there must
be room for some sentiment. It is quite ludicrous, if not bloody
mean, that players – and I have known it happen to former
Test players, who have given fine service to cricket and who
have been the idols of the Members' enclosures – have had to

go on to a waiting list, when their playing days were over, before they were eligible to pay for a membership. They are banished to the outfield.

You can put all this down, if you wish, to the crustiness of an old player but, before doing so, please remember it is the honest opinion of someone who has played longer than anyone else today.

I have tried to make a constructive contribution to cricket's problems in my own blunt – rough, if you like – way.

Thankfully, I have been fortunate enough to make many more friends than enemies in life and I hope to continue in the game for many more years. After all, I've still a long way to go to my 'ton'. . . .

Appendix

BILL ALLEY

Career Statistics compiled by Bill Frindall

1. ALL FIRST-CLASS MATCHES

A. BATTING AND FIELDING SUMMARY

SEASON	M.	I.	N.O.	RUNS	H.S.	AVGE.	100's	50's	CATCHES
1945–46	7	9	2	485	129*	69.28	3	–	2
1946–47	2	3	1	56	43*	28.00	–	–	–
1947–48	3	5	0	56	36	11.20	–	–	1
1949–50	18	28	9	1,255	209*	66.05	3	–	9
1953	1	2	0	15	11	7.50	–	–	–
1957	33	62	2	1,540	108	25.66	1	7	14
1958	31	58	2	1,318	89	23.53	–	9	24
1959	30	54	4	1,823	155	36.46	2	13	30
1960	27	42	7	807	110*	23.05	1	3	25
1961	35	64	11	3,019	221*	56.96	11	10	29
1962	23	58	6	1,915	155	36.82	3	12	27
1962–63 (CW)	2	4	0	133	54	33.25	–	1	1
1962–63 (CAV)	5	9	0	232	77	25.77	–	2	2
1963	25	38	2	1,076	105	29.88	1	5	17
1963–64	3	5	1	122	68	30.50	–	1	–
1964	29	47	3	1,332	140	30.27	1	6	25
1965	29	48	6	861	110	20.50	1	3	20
1966	30	51	3	1,104	115	23.00	2	4	26
1967	28	46	4	1,244	136	29.61	1	7	27
1968	29	49	4	1,219	110	27.08	1	6	14
	390	682	67	19,612	221*	31.88	31	89	293

* (*Not Out*)

B. BOWLING SUMMARY

SEASON	BALLS	MAIDENS	RUNS	WKTS	AVGE	5 WKTS INNS	10 WKTS MATCH
1945–46	224	3	118	2	59.00	–	–
1946–47	56	0	42	0	–	–	–
1947–48	136	2	59	3	19.33	–	–
1949–50	366	20	138	0	–	–	–
1953	276	6	120	1	120.00	–	–
1957	3,436	144	1,412	71	19.88	4	1
1958	3,115	113	1,257	56	22.44	3	–
1959	3,123	115	1,358	58	23.41	1	–
1960	4,386	206	1,679	73	23.00	5	–
1961	3,745	175	1,571	62	25.33	–	–
1962	5,689	254	2,323	112	20.74	6	–
1962–63 (CW)	120	2	92	2	46.00	–	–
1962–63 (CAV)	420	18	184	4	46.00	–	–
1963	2,406	148	758	39	19.43	2	–
1963–64	18	0	10	0	–	–	–
1964	3,904	213	1,365	64	21.32	4	–
1965	4,644	273	1,525	76	20.06	1	–
1966	3,114	170	1,015	50	20.30	2	–
1967	3,671	214	1,166	59	19.76	2	–
1968	3,143	184	1,229	36	34.13	–	–
	45,992	2,260	17,421	768	22.68	30	1

C. OVERSEAS CRICKET

1945–46 to 1947–48 inclusive:	New South Wales in Australia.
1949–50	Commonwealth in India, Pakistan and Ceylon.
1962–63	Commonwealth in Rhodesia.
1962–63	Cavaliers in South Africa and Rhodesia.
1963–64	Commonwealth in Pakistan.

D. FULL LIST OF HUNDREDS (31)

1945–46 (3)

111   New South Wales v. South Australia at Adelaide.
119   New South Wales v. Australian Services at Sydney.
129*   New South Wales v. South Australia at Sydney.

1949–50 (3)

168*   Commonwealth v. Indian Services XI at New Delhi (Irwin Stadium).
209*   Commonwealth v. West Zone at Poona.
206*   Commonwealth v. Cricket Club of India at Bombay.

1957 (1)

108   Somerset v. Worcestershire at Worcester.

1959 (2)

155   Somerset v. Gloucestershire at Taunton.
103   Somerset v. Glamorgan at Weston-super-Mare.

1960 (1)

110*   Somerset v. Sussex at Taunton.

* (*Not Out*)

1961 (11)

221*   Somerset *v.* Warwickshire at Nuneaton.

183* ⎫
134* ⎭   Somerset *v.* Surrey at Taunton.

123*   Somerset *v.* Nottinghamshire at Worksop.
134   Somerset *v.* Australians at Taunton.
155*   Somerset *v.* Yorkshire at Taunton.
156   Somerset *v.* Northamptonshire at Northampton.
117   Somerset *v.* Essex at Weston-super-Mare.
150*   Somerset *v.* Surrey at The Oval.
120   Somerset *v.* Lancashire at Bath.
102   A. E. R. Gilligan's XI *v.* Australians at Hastings.

1962 (3)

155   Somerset *v.* Kent at Gravesend.
102   Somerset *v.* Gloucestershire at Taunton.
131*   Somerset *v.* Lancashire at Glastonbury.

1963 (1)

105   Somerset *v.* Kent at Gillingham.

1964 (1)

140   Somerset *v.* Derbyshire at Chesterfield.

1965 (1)

110   Somerset *v.* Northamptonshire at Northampton.

1966 (2)

115   Somerset *v.* Nottinghamshire at Nottingham.
110*   Somerset *v.* Glamorgan at Taunton.

1967 (1)

136   Somerset *v.* Worcestershire at Glastonbury.

1968 (1)

110   Somerset *v.* Kent at Weston-super-Mare.

Alley scored hundreds against each of Somerset's County Championship opponents with the exception of Hampshire, Leicestershire and Middlesex.

E.   BEST BOWLING PERFORMANCES:

   1.   SIX OR MORE WICKETS IN AN INNINGS (9)

       8–65 Somerset *v.* Surrey at The Oval, 1962.
       7–58 Somerset *v.* Sussex at Weston-super-Mare, 1966.
       6–22 Somerset *v.* Hampshire at Bournemouth, 1957.
       6–39 Somerset *v.* Leicestershire at Leicester, 1958.
       6–40 Somerset *v.* Hampshire at Bath, 1965.
       6–42 Somerset *v.* Leicestershire at Ashby-de-la-Zouch, 1962.
       6–48 Somerset *v.* Nottinghamshire at Nottingham, 1962.
       6–63 Somerset *v.* Yorkshire at Bradford, 1967.
       6–116 Somerset *v.* Worcestershire at Bristol (Imperial Ground), 1964.

   2.   TEN WICKETS IN A MATCH (1)

       10–61 (4–39 and 6–22) Somerset *v.* Hampshire at Bournemouth, 1957.

F.   ALL-ROUND ACHIEVEMENTS

In 1962, Alley completed the Double of 1,000 runs and 100 wickets. He is

* (*Not Out*)

only the sixth Somerset player to do the Double, the others being: L. C. Braund (1901, 1902 and 1903), J. C. White (1929 and 1930), A. W. Wellard (1933, 1935 and 1937), W. H. R. Andrews (1937 and 1938), and K. E. Palmer (1961). With 1,915 runs (average 36.82) and 112 wickets (average 20.74), Alley was only 85 runs short of becoming the first Somerset player to do the rare double of 2,000 runs and 100 wickets.

Playing against Leicestershire at Ashby-de-la-Zouch in 1962, Alley dominated the game as a bowler, batsman and substitute wicket-keeper. In a low-scoring match, he scored 44 and 26 not out (including the winning hit) and bowled 55.5 overs for match figures of 9 for 95.

G. MEMORABILIA

In 1961, Alley set new county records for Somerset by scoring 2,761 runs (average 56.82) and 10 hundreds. In three matches between June 7th and 16th, he scored 523 runs in 5 innings for once out: 183* and 134* v. Surrey (Taunton), 13 run out and 70* v. Middlesex (Lord's), 123* v. Nottinghamshire (Worksop).

His partnership of 265 with K. E. Palmer against Northamptonshire at Northampton in 1961 set a new Somerset record for the sixth wicket.

By scoring 183* and 134* against Surrey at Taunton in 1961, Alley became the first Somerset player to score two not out centuries in a match. In the return game of that season at The Oval, he scored 150* and 9* to give an aggregate of 476 runs against Surrey in 1961 without being dismissed. The following season he again illustrated his partiality for the London county by taking 8 for 65: his best innings analysis in first-class matches.

Playing against Hampshire at Bath in 1965, Alley bowled unchanged throughout both innings: 20–7–34–2 and 26–9–40–6. Two seasons later he bowled unchanged for 35 overs to take 6 for 63 against Yorkshire at Bradford.

2. GILLETTE CUP MATCHES

Alley played in all of Somerset's first 16 Gillette Cup matches from 1963 to 1968 inclusive; ten of the games being won.

In the 1967 Final, he won a Runners-up Medal when Somerset were beaten by Kent, and on three occasions was awarded the Man of the Match Gold Medal and cheque:

    1966   38* and 4–14 v. Sussex at Taunton.
    1967   45 and 3–24 v. Warwickshire at Birmingham.
    1967   30 and 2–8 in 12 overs v. Northamptonshire at Northampton.

The two awards in 1967 came in successive rounds of the competition and his analysis of 12 overs for 8 runs against Northamptonshire is the most economic spell of bowling in the first six years of the Competition.

Alley's full Gillette Cup record is as follows:

BATTING:	MATCHES	INNINGS	NOT OUT	RUNS	H.S.	AVERAGE	50's
	16	16	2	281	58*	20.07	1

BOWLING:	OVERS	MAIDENS	RUNS	WICKETS	RUNS/WKT	RUNS/OVER	BEST
	184.1	56	405	25	16.20	2.19	4–14

* (Not Out)

INDEX

157